The Institute

The Institute

Virginia Military Institute

Photographed by
Anthony Edgeworth

Text by Geoffrey Norman

PUBLISHED BY EDGEWORTH EDITIONS
Copyright © 1997 by The VMI Foundation, Inc.
Photographs copyright © 1997 by Anthony Edgeworth
Text copyright © 1997 by Geoffrey Norman
This book was produced by
COMMONPLACE BOOKS, New Canaan, Connecticut
ART DIRECTOR: Samuel N. Antupit
EDITOR: Paul De Angelis
DESIGNER: Tania Garcia

The photographs for this book were taken with CANON cameras
using lenses ranging in size from 20mm to 600mm.

Printed in Hong Kong through Printnet

ISBN # 0-9658904-0-6— Library of Congress Card #: 97–90537

Any inquiries should be directed to:

Edgeworth Editions
2134 Polo Gardens Drive
Suite 104
Wellington, FL 33414

Frontispiece section photographs:

Lowering the flag at Retreat.

The Corps on the parade ground, autumn Friday.

The color guard.

Forage cap worn by Stonewall Jackson during many of his
famed Civil War campaigns; similar to the one he wore at VMI.
The background is an actual Confederate battle flag.
From the VMI Museum.

Rats on the fourth stoop. Second day of Cadre Week.

Having served in combat, under fire, VMI is the only cadet corps
authorized to parade with fixed bayonets.

At VMI, you march to meals.

Color guard's cartridge box.

Front endpaper:

The Institute, from downtown Lexington.

Back endpaper:

Statue of Stonewall Jackson: "The Institute will be heard from today."

Contents

❖

The Ratline and the Old Corps

❖

It is always an imposing sight: the stern, ocher face of Old Barracks; the parade ground; the cannon and the flags. It brings to mind a frontier fortress from the nineteenth century, an outpost. Whether you are a visitor, a cadet returning from leave, or even a loyal alumnus who has seen it a hundred times before, it still strikes you when you come back. It is clean, functional, and austere. Where the grounds at a typical four year college or university are typically called "the campus," at VMI, it is "the Post," and that fits perfectly.

In theory the Post could be anywhere, but it is impossible to imagine it except where it is — in Lexington, Virginia, up the Shenandoah Valley between the Blue Ridge and Allegheny mountains. The Valley is that part of Virginia least touched by the advances and architecture of the present. The farms and small towns in the Valley have the look and feel of another, more patient, more pastoral time: big barns, generous pastures where healthy looking horses graze idly, white clapboard churches with tall, imposing steeples, narrow streets, small shops, dignified old homes where the same families have lived for generations.

Lexington itself is as much old Virginia as it is contemporary America. It is a small, tidy college town where the streets are shaded by old, spreading hardwood trees and the homes have tall ceilings and wide porches that speak of an age before air conditioning. The town seems, in its way, as much a part of the unchanging landscape as House Mountain, which looms over everything a mile or so to the west.

The American past is very present in Lexington, particularly a painful, tragic part of that past. The American Civil War is barely a schoolbook memory in much of the country. But in Lexington, where two of the Confederacy's greatest generals are buried, the Civil War is impossible to ignore or forget. The cemetery in town hosts the grave of "Stonewall" Jackson, who taught at VMI before the war, while Robert E. Lee is interred in the chapel on the grounds of Washington & Lee University, the school that bears his name and where he served as President in the last years of his life.

So the Post, which would stand out like a medieval fortress in any other American town, does not seem incongruous here in Lexington. The formidably high, battlemented parapets of Old Barracks are striking enough, but somehow they seem to fit in with the surroundings. The barracks was built on the site of the original arsenal, established by the state of Virginia in 1816. Soldiers who guarded this arsenal sometimes caused trouble in town, so in the mid 1830s the state of Virginia decided to establish a school on the same location, a school where young men would be both educated in

Opposite page:

From high school hero to VMI zero." A young man arrives through Jackson Arch prior to matriculation.

the traditional sense and trained as soldiers. They would also guard the arsenal. In 1839, that school took in its first class of twenty-three cadets. Cadet guards still walk sentry duty around the Post, though the arsenal has been closed since 1864.

The original Old Barracks was shelled and burned by Union troops, in retaliation for the cadets' performance during the battle of New Market during the last year of the Civil War. It was painstakingly rebuilt in its former image after the war. With its formidable facade and the large arch that serves as an entryway, it is the first thing that draws the eye of a visitor. There is a statue of Thomas Jonathan "Stonewall" Jackson in front of the arch named for Jackson. To the north of Old Barracks is an annex, New Barracks, built in 1949. In front of its entryway, called Marshall Arch, stands a statue of General George C. Marshall, who graduated from VMI in 1901 and went on to command all American forces in World War II and, then, win a Nobel Peace Prize as Secretary of State.

A vast, twelve-acre parade ground stretches out in front of the barracks, and around the parade ground stand other buildings, all built in the same castellated Gothic style and painted the same austere, sandy yellow. Some of these are academic buildings. Some are quarters for the Superintendent, the Commandant, and other members of the faculty. On the right flank of Old Barracks is Jackson Memorial Hall, the chapel, which was completed in 1916. Money for construction came from funds voted by the United States government to compensate VMI for damage done during the Civil War. Senator Henry A. DuPont of Delaware was instrumental in securing the appropriation. He had wanted to attend VMI himself, but could not because he was not from Virginia. He fought on the Union side during the Civil War, and at the battle of New Market, against cadets from VMI. There is history everywhere you look on the Post.

The Post is never more imposing than in the eyes of the young man who arrives in August to begin his four years at VMI. When he comes through the Limits Gate to enroll officially, he will survey the grounds and the buildings and inevitably ask himself whether he can measure up to the sense of purpose and mission they seem to suggest. One reason he is here is to answer that question. A young man who enters VMI puts the old, familiar world behind him. It is almost as though he has taken vows. If he is faithful to them, if he makes it, he will become part of the brotherhood — and then the buildings and the grounds of the Post will be beautiful in his eyes as well as imposing, and the best part of him will always be here.

The first step on the way to becoming part of that brotherhood is "matriculation." When the young man signs in the book, his name will join those of men like George S. Patton Jr., Lewis "Chesty" Puller, George C. Marshall, and hundreds of others who have gone on to glory.

After he has signed the book, the young man and his parents enter Jackson Memorial Hall for a welcoming address by the Superintendent. Nearly four hundred young men attend this ceremony, along with many parents who have come to see their sons off. This speech is the last event they will share. From now on, each young man will be on his own. There is some sense of this in the air. The mood at JM Hall, as it's called, is solemn. These could be church services.

Josiah Bunting III, the thirteenth VMI Superintendent, is introduced and makes a short speech. Bunting is a VMI graduate, '63, Rhodes Scholar, combat veteran, and author: a modern Renaissance man who wears his uniform and decorations with assurance.

"We welcome you," Bunting says to the new men, "to a special place. A place that will, in time, mean as much to you as to all the men who have gone before you."

That includes the New Market cadets, whose Civil War charge is depicted in a large, vivid painting on the wall behind Bunting. As the new men and their parents listen to Bunting's words, some of them are no doubt thinking that this is not merely the next stage in life. On this day, at this place, a young man opens one door and closes many more behind him.

"Parents," says another VMI officer, after Bunting has finished speaking, "please say good-bye to your sons now."

There are hugs around JM Hall. And many tears.

After he has signed his name and said his farewells, the young man goes through two days of admissions and familiarization that are, in many ways, similar to what is going on at hundreds of other schools all around the country. This is the administrative period, before the actual school year and classes begin. He is tested. He is advised. He is enrolled in courses. VMI is, after all, a college. The boys he went to high school with, young men who look like the other new VMI students, are doing the same thing at other schools. Deciding how many hours to take as a freshman and what language to study. It is no different here.

But things are going on all around him, on the Post, that are very different. Men who don't look at all like ordinary college students are out on the parade ground, working. They wear camouflage pants, black boots, black baseball hats, and black t-shirts with the word "Cadre" spelled out on the chest. And where a few upper class students who have returned early at a typical college will be playing softball or throwing a frisbee in the hot, late summer afternoon, these men are doing close order drill. Marching. Standing at attention and parade rest. They do not look like students at all. They look like soldiers; and very serious soldiers at that. There is nothing lighthearted or frivolous in what they are doing, and as the young man moves from building to building on his way through the orientation and enrollment process, he looks over at them and thinks about what is coming next. If he knows anything at all about VMI, he knows about the Cadre.

Other cadets in white uniform pants and shirt escort the new men around the Post in groups. These are "S-5" cadets, and while the new man doesn't know enough yet to understand the designation, he is quick to pick up on the fact that they are relatively friendly and approachable, unlike the men he sees in black t-shirts and black baseball hats, practicing close order drill.

The S-5 escorts point out the landmarks and describe their significance. They take the new men for uniform issue and fitting. There is nothing like this business of uniforms at a typical college or university, and the new men will learn a lot about uniforms, and how to wear them, in the next few weeks. For now, they are measured and fitted and issued camouflage fatigues (Battle Dress Uniform is the official term, or BDUs) and athletic gear. The new men are also escorted to another stop that would not be part of a typical college indoctrination: the barber shop. Here, in less than five minutes, the new man loses all his hair. It is quick and impersonal, and it leaves him feeling like a man who has lost some important part of his identity. All high school boys worry about their hair and spend time fussing with it. Now, suddenly, there is no hair. None at all. And soon there won't be time to fuss with it anyway.

Following pages:

In JM Hall, after matriculation and after the speeches. "Parents, please say good-bye to your sons."

New men, forming up in Jackson Arch.

Cadre cadets Pridgen, Moder, Zoffuto, and Smith. The Rats will come to know them well.

Rats' Day One

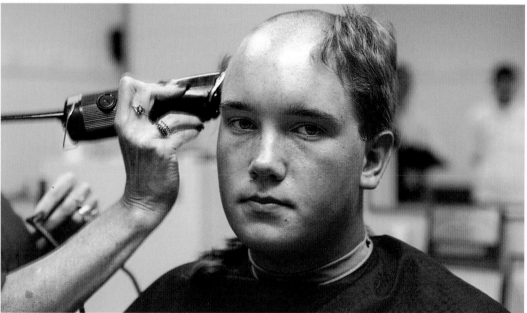

Right:

A *man loses his hair and his civilian identity . . . and becomes a Rat.*

Standing outside the barber shop, the new man looks around at the other men with their naked scalps and wonders if he looks as grotesque as they do. Without hair, they all look like freshly hatched birds. And more importantly, they all look alike.

He knows some of these other men a little, since he has been assigned to a room with three of them and they have talked. Their room on the fourth stoop (floor, in civilian language) of the barracks is furnished with desks and open lockers and a cot, or rack, that folds up and down for storage. The wooden furniture is as Spartan as everything else at VMI and has been built, appropriately enough, by prison labor.

No hair; wooden furniture built by convicts. The new man has already come a long way from the life of his old friends who have gone off to more conventional colleges and universities where there are rugs on dormitory floors and students are accustomed to the usual conveniences — telephones, televisions, stereos. The new VMI man is given a mattress for his rack and learns first that it is called a "hay," and then, that he is expected to roll it up and store it every morning. He must also fold the wooden cot and store it, in the prescribed manner, against the wall. In the unlikely event that he has any free time during the day, he will not spend it lying in bed listening to the stereo, talking on the phone, or watching television.

The comforts that he has become accustomed to are now a thing of the past. And that is the easy part.

Two nights after he has arrived at VMI, as he lies on his hay in his room on the fourth stoop of Barracks, listening to the agitated breathing of his sleeping roommates, the new man will inevitably think of the next chapter in his new, unsettling life. The moment when he meets the Cadre. He knows it is coming. Tomorrow afternoon, right after lunch. What he cannot know and what worries him so much that he cannot sleep is this — is he ready?

Matriculation was Monday morning. On Wednesday afternoon, the real life of new VMI men begins.

They are dressed in gym shorts, t-shirts, and athletic shoes. "Gym dyke," this outfit is called. ("Dyke" is a multi-purpose word at VMI. In this context, it means "uniform.")

It is late in August and hot in the Shenandoah Valley of Virginia, and this day seems especially, almost relentlessly hot. The S-5 escorts bring the new men into the courtyard of New Barracks and line them up, in loose ranks against the steel pipe railing around first stoop, facing the center of the courtyard. As the new men come into the courtyard, they are greeted by the jeering, taunting voices of cadets on the second and third stoops who have come to watch somebody else get what they once had to live through. These cadets are athletes, members of the band, and others who have returned early from the summer break. The majority of upper classmen — the Old Corps — will not return for another ten days.

For ten minutes or more, the new men stand, packed in ranks and waiting. From above, the cadets jeer and shout.

"You're going to get it now, Rat."

"You'd better buckle your chin strap, Rat. Here it comes."

"You're going to love this, you sorry Rat."

The escorts instruct the new men, some of whose knees are trembling, to begin clapping. They clap. And the rhythm of their clapping echoes loudly through the courtyard. Urged on by their escorts, the Rats begin chanting.

"We want Cadre. We want Cadre."

Which inspires the cadets on the stoops to jeer even louder.

Now the escorts tell the men to chant something new.

"Brother Rat. Brother Rat."

They are barely Rats, in fact, and none of them know each other — even roommates — well enough to think of themselves as brothers. Not yet, though that will come. But right now, crowded into the courtyard and suffering under the heat, the jeers, and the anticipation, they are getting the first taste of what it means to be Brother Rats. What it comes down to, fundamentally, is shared suffering.

They clap and they chant and the noise fills the courtyard.

"Brother Rat. Brother Rat."

And then, over the chants and the clapping, comes the pounding of a bass drum, heavy and ominous. The clapping and the chanting and the jeering die out and, except for the drum, the courtyard is momentarily silent.

From the courtyard of Old Barracks, through the connecting passageway that the Rats will learn is called "the Sally port," come two long ranks of men, marching slowly to keep cadence with the drums. There is something almost grave in the rhythm of their steps and the drum.

The men are dressed in starched white pants and gray wool tunics ("gray blouse," the uniform is called) and they look stiff, formal, hot, and uncomfortable. Also very serious. More serious, as they say, than a heart attack.

The two long ranks proceed down the courtyard of New Barracks, between the two tight masses of new men. None of the men in white and gray look to either side. Their eyes are fixed forward. When they are all the way inside the courtyard and aligned with the masses of new men, they halt. Then each rank turns to face the new men, who are packed against the steel railings that separate the courtyard from the passageway around the first stoop.

The drum falls silent. There is, for a moment, no sound in the hot, still afternoon air. The men in gym dyke face the men in dress uniform. All of the men in uniform look straight ahead. One man's lips twitch and quiver with anticipation.

On the second stoop, at the end of the New Barracks, a cadet — dressed like the rest of the Cadre in white trousers and gray blouse, no hat — steps up to the steel railing and speaks words that anyone who has ever been a Rat can remember and probably recite.

"Rats, this is your Cadre. They are the best. They will teach. And you will learn. Rats —" and here there is a long pause before the words that are the beginning of a completely new experience, " . . . meet your Cadre."

What follows next is inevitably described this way by those who have been through it: All hell breaks loose.

The men in uniform charge into the ranks of men in shorts and t-shirts. They get close. Very close. Right in the faces of men they have picked out. And they scream.

"What are you looking at, Rat? What are you looking at? Are you looking at me? Don't you look at me. Don't you ever look at me. You keep your worthless eyes straight ahead. . . . What did you say? You better say "Sir" when you talk to me, Rat . . . . Get down on your face and push. Down . . . get down."

Fingers punch in the air in front of the Rats' trembling faces and hot, raucous words grate on their ears. The Rats are down to do pushups. Up to run in place. The din of the screaming and the jeers of the cadets from the upper stoops is like the noise from a crowd at a football game that has lost control. Too deafening for anyone to think, especially a Rat. The best you can do if you're a Rat is to scream "Yes, sir" and "No sir," and get down on your face and knock out those pushups. For the Rat, it is bedlam. Insanity. And it seems to go on forever.

"I didn't even know where I was, after a while," one bewildered young man says at the end of the day. "I mean, it was just crazy. I knew it was going to be bad. But I didn't know it was going to be like that."

It does not go on forever. Nobody could last. Within fifteen or twenty minutes, the Rats are formed up by companies — their old high school buddies choose fraternities while they are assigned to companies — and move out. To their rooms, to the parade ground, to various stations around the Post where they will be at the mercies of the Cadre.

It is August and the heat bears down like a weight. Cadre members make it back to their rooms for a quick change to BDU trousers and black t-shirts. In this uniform, they look even more intimidating. And intimidate is what they do, for the rest of the afternoon.

Each Rat has a Rat Bible, officially called *The Bullet*. Rats are responsible for everything in the Rat Bible. They may not yet know what the parts of an M-14 rifle are (they soon will) but they had better know that this year's Rat Disciplinary Committee president is Cadet Jeffrey Staub. If they don't, they pay.

"Get down, Rat. On your face. On your face and push."

So when they are not learning how to pop to attention when somebody slams open the door to their room, or to march in step or execute a right face properly, they are learning about the Ratline, that imaginary straight line along the stoops. (Each floor of the barracks is a stoop, and on each "stoop" there is a passageway, almost a landing, that is about five feet wide.) On the stoops and stairs, Rats must walk the imaginary line at the outer edge of the stoop. And they must cut square corners. If there is an upper classman in the way they must ask "permission to go around sir," and wait until it is given. This invisible course is the technical definition of the Ratline, but the term is applied to all that the Rats must do and know. They are in the Ratline as long as they are Rats.

The groups of Rats move everywhere at a rapid cadence, called "driving on," along the Ratline. Awkward and stiff, as though with fear, which is certainly part of it. When they are not driving on, they are doing pushups or mountain climbers or . . . running, but not to get anywhere, just running in place.

Always, they are being yelled at. From very close range. There's a six inch rule at VMI. But nobody ever measures.

The Rats do not have the time, or the composure, to wonder why this is happening. But it is a question that any spectator — even one of the cadets who's returned early or a member of the Cadre or the administration — might ask. What is the point of all this? Is it merely, as some of VMI's critics insist (and there are many of them), a refined example of adolescent sadism — fraternity hazing raised to a higher level? Is it really nothing more than a ritualized bullying that serves no purpose other than to make those who have endured it feel that they have passed some kind of initiation into a secret society?

VMI men and supporters will tell you there is a point to all this, and a profound and important purpose. VMI is a military school; not merely a four year college where the students happen to wear uniforms and drill. The military mission is the soul of VMI. It has turned out thousands of citizen soldiers, many of whom have served, and continue to serve, with great distinction. The ethos of VMI is a military one, that of the warrior culture. And before a man can become a soldier he must first cease being an individual. He must be broken down and then built up. He must be tested. He must learn discipline and obedience. He must learn to do more than he thought he could do and endure more than he thought he could endure.

All military elites test those who want to join their ranks. Before a civilian can become a Marine, he must pass through the rigors of boot camp. Before a soldier can become a paratrooper, he must go through the ordeal of airborne school. Before a sailor can become a SEAL he must survive "Hell Week." And before the men who have so recently matriculated at VMI can even become an official class—the first class of the new century, the class of 2000, and incidentally the last all male class at VMI—they must go through Cadre Week and, then, the Ratline, which will last until spring. Until then, they are not a class, they are merely a "Rat mass."

Cadre Week is the time of testing. It begins with awesome, shocking suddenness. The time of building will be much slower and last much longer. It will last, in fact, four long years.

In the first hours of the first day, heat, fatigue, anxiety, and a frantic pace all begin to wear down some of the softer bodies and weaker wills. Before one Rat is a full hour into an ordeal that will last more than six months, he is face down in a pool of his own vomit. Cadet EMTs (Emergency Medical Technicians) are stationed around the Post and two of them hurry to the scene. Eventually the man is evacuated to the hospital and given fluids. He will be back and, in fact, he will make it all the way through the Ratline.

Others cannot wait to leave. Every Rat wonders if he will make it and there are a few, on this first afternoon in the worst year of their lives, who decide not to draw out the suspense. They want out. In a hurry. Right now is not soon enough.

There is a room on the first stoop next to the Commandant's office, just off Jackson Arch, where they go to quit. Before they can leave, however, they are counseled. First by members of the S-5 staff, some of the same cadets who have been escorting them solicitously around the Post for the last two days. These are the friendly cadets. The good cops to the Cadre's bad cops. They talk to you, instead of screaming at you.

"Come on over here and let's talk," one says to a bewildered looking Rat, his skinned head slick with sweat and his t-shirt filthy where he has collapsed onto the ground, too exhausted to do another pushup.

"You can do this. It is just something to get through. Everybody you see here, everybody in this room, has been through it. I got through it. . . . "

He leaves the rest unsaid. He and the Rat leave the room to take a walk and talk it over along those lines: "If I can get through it, then so can you."

But some can't. Or don't want to, which amounts to the same thing. And when counseling by one of the S-5 cadets has failed, the disenchanted Rat has a talk with Doc Monsour, VMI's all-purpose wise man and school counselor.

"I can turn some of them around by reminding them that they wanted to be here, and if they make it through today, then they can make it through tomorrow," he says, "but some of them just want to quit and nothing on earth could keep them here."

Leaving is easy but not exactly simple. After cadet counseling and a talk with Doc

Monsour, the Rat who wants out must talk to the Deputy Commandant, the Commandant, and the Dean. And he must call home.

There are fathers who, when the call comes, tell the Commandant, "You keep him until I get there. I'll be right down."

But some young men are going to leave. No matter what.

"No matter how much you think you're ready for it," they say around VMI, "there is no way you can be."

Four or five men will be gone by the end of the first day. More than a dozen by the time classes begin, in another ten days. More than forty — ten percent of the class — by the time the Rats are given their first taste of leave at Thanksgiving.

This process of attrition is harsh but necessary. Admission to the brotherhood comes in stages and at each stage, some are left behind. You cannot be a VMI man unless you have made it and that means that some young men won't make it . . . that some will be gone before the end of the first really rough day.

There is no reliable way of knowing who will make it and who won't. Some men who look frail and physically inadequate will make it on sheer will power. They will go down on their faces and do as many pushups as they can, then endure the screams to keep on going when they no longer can, while some men who plainly have the physical makeup are missing the most necessary ingredient: a toughness and determination that only the experience itself will unveil. Certainly, it is not simple physical durability, though being in shape helps. One of the men who reports to the S-5 Cadets and Doc Monsour to begin outprocessing on the first day has come to VMI to play lacrosse. You can look at him and see that pushups are not the problem.

"Some of them think that it is going to be strenuous like team practice in sports," one of the S-5 cadets says, sympathetically. "They aren't ready for the mental pressure. Maybe they never even thought about it. Some of them are actually surprised. They had no idea what it would really be like."

But then, he continues, there are some men who come knowing as much as it is possible to know and still do not last. "There was one, a couple of years ago. His father was a graduate and some kind of important officer in the alumni association. The kid had visited VMI before he enrolled and he was hot to come here. Then, two days after he meets the Cadre, he quits. 'I just never knew it was going to be like this,' he said. And that's true. There's no way he could have known."

Five new men leave on this first day, and a few report to the infirmary. Some of these come back wearing white tags on their t-shirts. These tags excuse a man from arduous duty. While his Brother Rats do pushups, he stands and watches.

A man who wears one of those tags is on the "Gim." The tag, therefore, is a "Gim sheet." The term comes from the misty past, when the Post surgeon's assistant made his rounds in a wagon drawn by a horse named Gimlet. Cadets on the sick list were said to be "riding the Gim." The phrase became a part of a language known only to VMI men.

These days, "riding the Gim" translates roughly as goldbricking. No cadet wants to be accused of it. To fake an injury to avoid duty is a form of lying — an honor violation, about which the Rats will learn much more as time goes by. But to ride the Gim as a way to duck the strains of the Ratline is a kind of betrayal of the men you are already thinking of as your "Brother Rats."

This makes for an interesting irony. "Malingering is not really a big problem," says Dr. Copeland, the school physician, who keeps himself close to the S-5 room during the first days, in case he is needed. "But the opposite thing — call it counter-malingering — is a problem and sometimes a serious one. I'll see one of these Rats limping and ask him what's the matter and he'll say, 'Nothing, sir.' When I examine him, I'll find an injury — a sprained ankle or a knee, say — that is easily bad enough for him to go on the Gim. And he'll beg me to let him stay in the Ratline. Happens all the time."

The idea of hiding an injury so that you can take part in the group harrassment of Cadre Week may seem perverse to someone who doesn't know VMI. But that is part of the spirit. You want to share the ordeal with your Brother Rats. Some Rats have already absorbed so much of the VMI spirit that standing in the Gim line while their Brother Rats are knocking out pushups seems almost unendurable, even when they are on crutches. They seem almost ashamed of the paper tags that flutter from their shirts like badges of shame.

One of the first lessons of VMI is unity. The worst feeling is to be separate and isolated from your Brother Rats . . . especially when they are suffering. Those who do not find being on the Gim more painful than the injury that put them there probably do not belong at VMI. The Cadre have an unerring feel for the Rats who are pleased to be on the Gim, and will be waiting when they return.

At the end of the first day, after some Rats have quit, some men are on the Gim, and the rest have fallen onto their hays stunned and exhausted, the members of the Cadre gather in their rooms on the first three stoops where they talk in voices that are strained and hoarse, in spite of the throat lozenges that the EMTs have been passing out to them all day.

If the Rats are stunned, the Cadre cadets are serene. They knew exactly what to expect from this day and have been rehearsing for it, even looking forward to it.

VMI needs the Cadre cadets as much as it needs the Rats. It is one of the strengths of the Institute — of the "I" — that the Cadre does what it does so well. The Cadre is the soul of the regimental system, the purely military side of cadet life at VMI. The regimental system constitutes a sphere of authority apart and different from that of the Class System, the Honor System, and the administration.

For the Rats the mix of authority structures is at first bewildering, especially since some of them overlap. Where does the Class System begin and the regimental system end? What is the role of the administration? How does the Honor System fit in? As the new cadets soon learn, the regimental system runs life in ranks, on the parade ground. The Class System, which they will learn about later, runs life in the barracks.

The emphasis during these first days is on the military side of life, the regimental system as represented by the Cadre. The Cadre is made up of the cadet corporals, sergeants — the noncoms — and officers from all three upper classes. These men have rank, which they wear on their sleeves, and they are generally the most militarily minded of the cadets. Many have come to VMI to earn a commission and become career officers. They believe in the necessity of Cadre Week for VMI in the same way a Parris Island drill instructor believes in boot camp as essential for the Marine Corps.

"I don't look at it as personal," says one. "It's a job and I want to do the best job I can. This is what VMI is all about; why it is not just another college. If you don't want

Opposite page:

The heat and the strain gets to some men. But a few hours after some medical attention most Rats, like this one, are back in the Ratline.

to do this, then you shouldn't come here. We do this and, if we are going to do it, then we ought to do it right."

The man who says this — and he could be speaking for the entire Cadre — is one of those third class corporals. Within the Institute, third class corporals are a legend. They were Rats just a few months ago. They have lusted for their chance and now they have it. They love the military side of VMI life. They are the hard cases.

"Oh, maybe," says one who is spending the evening listening to music and spit shining his boots. "But I'm not some sadist. Like I said, I'm doing my job. VMI is supposed to be tough. It is supposed to be military. This is why people come here."

Like this man, many cadets want as much of the military experience as they can get . . . more even than they can get during the school year. While the boys they went to high school with are traveling around Europe, climbing in the Rockies, or working at summer jobs, they are doing the things military men do. This man spent part of his summer vacation at Fort Benning, Georgia, where he went to Airborne School and got his jump wings. Lots of running and pushups and, then, five jumps.

After VMI, he says, "it was easy."

Among the Cadre, there are men who spent the last summer at Quantico, Virginia going through the Marine Corps Officer Candidate School. Or at Tyndall Air Force Base, where at least two cadets saw a recent VMI graduate almost finish qualifying in the F-15s and decided, no doubt seeing some of themselves in him, to make F-15s their career choice as well. Or with the Navy at Norfolk, Virginia. One of the officers assigned to the NROTC unit at VMI is, himself, a graduate of VMI who knew very little about the military and especially about the Navy when he arrived in Lexington from Kansas. He found his calling — nuclear submarines — during one of his summer cruises.

"VMI men do real well in the nuke program," he says. "It takes brains but it also takes discipline."

Men who trained first at VMI serve across the spectrum of U.S. military forces — from the infantry, to fighter planes, to fast attack nuclear submarines. The Institute tradition of producing military leaders is strong enough to saturate the stones of the Post. The names Jackson, Marshall, and Lejeune are part of the daily vocabulary of VMI. Everywhere you look around the Post you see reminders of the contribution that VMI has made down the years — from the New Market dead buried under the statue of *Virginia Mourning Her Dead*, to the plaque in Lejeune Hall commemorating the two VMI men killed during the Gulf War. There are plaques outside Washington Arch listing those who fell in World War II. More plaques on the wall in the garden outside Cocke Hall, given by their Brother Rats to honor men who died in World War II, Korea, Vietnam. A room in the Library to honor the Vietnam dead, including one VMI graduate who was killed by communist guerrillas while he covered the invasion of Cambodia for United Press International.

The memorials are everywhere. You cannot pass through VMI unaware of them. The message strikes some VMI men more forcefully than others. These days there is no requirement to serve, as there was during the days of the Cold War and the draft, so more than half the men at VMI will never go to summer camp and will not be commissioned upon graduation.

In some way, this increases the ardor of those who do. It could be that they see themselves as custodians of the true spirit of VMI, which is in military service. Or it could

be that they are just gung ho and like to kick ass. Whatever, the Cadre cadets are passionate about what they do and dedicated to doing it right and not worried about hurting the feelings of any Rats who might be having a hard time adjusting.

"This is what it is all about," the third class corporal says, as he finishes spit shining the jump boots he will be wearing in the morning when he greets the Rats. "I mean, if you don't have this—the military part and the Rat Line—then it is just college. And you can get that anywhere. Right?"

For ten long, hot days the Cadre teaches. And the Rats learn. Or at least try. There is too much to absorb at once. The Rats learn their chain of command, their general orders, the customs and traditions of VMI. All of the material, in short, that is in the Rat Bible. Every one of them must be able to recite that information upon demand and without hesitation . . . while the person demanding it is screaming into his face. And they have to learn how to do the things all soldiers must learn how to do: the rudiments of drill, how to march in step, keep your interval and dress, do a left face and a right face, how to stand at attention and parade rest. It looks simple, but it turns out to be very, very hard, and mistakes are not tolerated.

"Left face, Rat. *Left* face. Your *other* left. Don't look at me, don't look at me. Just do it."

The days begin early, when someone from the Cadre slams the door of your room open, and screams at you to get up and get in formation in your gym clothes for a run. In the thin, moist early morning light, you run three miles in formation, clapping and chanting cadence. When Rats who are out of shape fall out, gasping for air and wobbling on exhausted legs, the Cadre is all over them. The first lesson of the day is that you cannot quit. No Rat is permitted to fall behind. There is no excuse. Failure is not permitted. No slack. If your Brother Rat cannot run with the rest of the platoon, the rest of you will have to carry him.

You are forced to do more than you thought you could. Run further. Do more pushups. Get by on less sleep. Learn more than you thought you could. All the names of the men on the Honor Court. The names of the members of the regimental commander and his staff. Your company commander and his staff. The New Market dead.

There is no relief and you cannot hide. Not even while you eat. At VMI, you do not look at your watch, decide you are hungry, and head off for something to eat. You march, in formation, to all meals. And if you are a Rat, you sit at attention in the mess hall, on the first three inches of your chair, and throughout the meal the Cadre cadets at either end of the table are shouting at you for answers.

"What is your first general order, Rat."

"I don't know sir," a Rat says helplessly, swallowing a mouthful of lumpy mashed potatoes—hot, unappetizing food on a heaving stomach. His eyes are fixed on some imaginary point in front of his face. He looks pale, uncomprehending, and exhausted. Too confused to eat or to understand the question.

"You don't know?" the Cadre corporal screams.

"No sir," the Rat answers miserably, around the forkful of potatoes. His eyes fill with tears.

"I'll see you outside, Rat. I've got my eye on you. I'm going to be watching you Rat. I'm going to be everywhere you go. I'm going to be on you like white on rice, Rat. You understand that? Do you understand that, Rat?"

"Yes sir."

"No you don't. You only think you do."

But as the long, hot days pass, the Rats learn. Some learn quickly. Others slowly. Some hardly at all. The Cadre spots these and is on them, closing in like predators on the weakest animals in a herd.

"You aren't going to make it, Rat. You know why?"

"No sir."

"Because you don't have what it takes. Maybe I'll be able to get you through. It'll be hard on me, but I can take it. The question is. . . can you?"

The days seem to last longer than any day possibly could and at night, when the Rats fall onto their hays, they feel stunned. And when the morning comes, with the door knocked open by a screaming Cadre cadet, it comes sooner than seems possible. Another day begins. More running and more PT and more drill and more things to learn. More shouted questions. More pushups.

But by the end of the week, the Rats are beginning to get it. Already some of the platoons are marching in step with a rhythm and snap to their step. They look different from the rough assortment of college kids they were when they arrived with their parents, their hair, and their uncertainties just a few days ago. This is the beginning of the process that has gone on here for a century and a half. The making of VMI men.

The Cadre teaches. The Rats learn.

The process is already well underway that first week, before classes have even begun or the Old Corps is back on the grounds. More than a dozen of the men who signed the book have already left. Others are on the edge of leaving. A few have already made themselves into something that resembles a VMI cadet. They have learned to march and to salute and to recite most of the fundamental things. And they are pulling their Brother Rats along. This mutual assistance is another element in the bond that slowly, arduously forms as each new year at VMI moves into gear.

At the end of the week, on Sunday, the Rats march out along Woods Creek — known as "the Nile" around VMI — to a picnic area for a cookout. It is the first chance they have had to relax since the drum began beating, that Friday afternoon, in what seems like another life a long time ago.

They eat grilled hot dogs and hamburgers ravenously — they have learned already about the mess hall food. They tell war stories about what they have already been through, one of the little pleasures of VMI life. They have already recognized the main "flamers" among the Cadre:

"So Zoffuto is in my face, screaming like a maniac. 'Get up, get down.' I didn't even know what he was saying. He's so close I could count his teeth."

Most of the Rats are already able to find the humor in these stories. Some listen but do not laugh while others, a few, keep to themselves. These solitaries are the ones to watch. There is still some attrition to come. But for now, these Rats have made it over the first obstacle, Cadre Week. The bond, though still weak, has been formed.

Meanwhile, some nine hundred other cadets have been arriving at the Post. They are upper classmen — the Old Corps — back from whatever it was they have been doing for the last three months, summer jobs or summer camp. The barracks, and the Post, have been returning to full life.

The returning men come back with a different set of expectations, depending upon the stoop where they live and the class to which they belong.

On the third stoop, the third classmen have returned knowing one thing above all—they are no longer Rats. It might not seem like much to anyone outside the VMI fraternity, but when you are a Rat, you are told over and over that you will be a Rat until you can see a Rat. Now that they have moved into rooms on the third stoop, they've crossed the line. For now, that is enough.

Their year won't be easy, however. (What year at VMI is?) The Institute is built around a class system and each class has its privileges. For now, it is enough merely not to be a Rat. But as the year wears on, thirds learn that VMI doesn't necessarily get easier. It just gets hard in a different way. After a summer of freedom, the Post and the barracks will quickly close in. They used to say that a third is "just a Rat with a radio." Third class privileges are scarce: a little more time off on weekends and a few occasions when they are allowed uptown. They can wear bathrobes on the stoop, but this is thin solace after the first month or two.

And classroom pressures will wear the thirds down. This year they will endure the "academic Ratline." They lost people last year who couldn't take it. This year, it will be the people who can't make it. Organic chemistry is just as tough whether you wear a uniform or blue jeans. But for now, on the first day back, it is enough to have Rats around you and not to be one yourself, and, to be reunited with your Brother Rats from last year.

Second classmen moving in on the second stoop have more to anticipate. For one thing, they have survived the two most demanding years. The attrition is not complete (some men leave, even, in the last weeks of their last year) but for the most part, the men who are still here will be here at graduation. Now they are looking not merely to survive but to get themselves ready for the next thing. This is the time to start polishing the resume, to concentrate on those things at VMI that will be important later. Men who plan to go on to graduate school, law school, or medical school know they have to make their grades and complete their required courses.

For the men whose eyes are on the military, this means working hard on those things that will get them the choice assignments. You need the grades for nuke school and you need the PT scores for summer mountain training. You need to get some cadet rank and show the Air Force or the Navy that you have the right stuff for flight training. Serious business.

And, for second classmen, this is the year when they will be formally admitted to the brotherhood, at Ring Figure. A committee, selected last year, has already completed the work of designing the ring.

For the first classmen, who lost their hair and their innocence here three years ago, the experience they have been waiting for has finally come. This is the year when their class will leave its mark on VMI. The first class runs life in the barracks through its officers—class president, vice president, and historian—the Rat Disciplinary Committee (which the Rats will come to know as the dreaded RDC), the General Committee, the Officers of the Guard Association.

All these student-run structures might bewilder a Rat or an outsider, but to the men now returning, the Old Corps, it makes perfect sense. It has for more than 150 years. All elements of the class system, the Ratline, and the regimental system were in place within a few months after the old arsenal at Lexington became VMI. It is a complicated hierarchy, completely understood only by those who have lived under its rule.

It is difficult for an outsider to understand or appreciate how fundamental the Class System is to life at VMI. If VMI is a brotherhood, then each class is a brotherhood within the larger one. The men you go through the Ratline with will always be your "Brother Rats." At reunions it is common to see men from their forties on up introducing wives and children to an old comrade as "my Brother Rat." That bond, first formed during Cadre Week, is probably at its strongest among first classmen. They have been through a lot together, and this is their moment.

"I've been looking forward to this," says Jeff Staub, president of the RDC, "for three years."

He makes it sound like a lifetime.

The course is set that first night after the Old Corps returns . . . or early the next morning to be exact, at about three hours before dawn. It's an hour at which the Rats have become accustomed to hear a foot on the door. This time, they are awakened by a blast of powder from "Little John," the Institute's ceremonial cannon, and two M-60 machine guns firing blanks. The courtyard is full of noise and smells—of black powder from the cannon, and cordite from the machine gun blanks.

"Get up Rats. Get up. Get in your gym dyke and get down in front of the barracks, in formation."

Pandemonium follows . . . pandemonium that is worse than anything that came before, and that already seemed about as bad as it could get.

Ten times as many angry voices shout at the Rats as have ever yelled at them before.

"Move, move, move. Get outside, get in formation. Close it up. Close it up. Move."

The Rats line up single file, the nose of one man touching the neck of the man in front of him, and march into JM Hall, where they were welcomed, along with their families, a couple of weeks earlier. This welcome will not be so cordial.

The president of the first class, Addison Hagan, marches down the center aisle, his steps echoing ominously through the hall. Hagan and the regimental commander, Brian Bagwan, have more power, responsibility, and respect than any other cadets on the Post. Hagan's father, grandfather, and great-grandfather are VMI graduates. So are several other relatives. His father was a Marine Corps officer in Vietnam, and also a first class president (1968). VMI is in Hagan's blood.

He comes right to the point in a speech that the cadets will never forget:

"You," Hagan says, glaring out at the Rats packed onto the benches in front of him, "are lower than a virus. The leaves are on the trees and you are in the Ratline. The leaves will fall and you will still be in the Ratline. Soon the snow will come and you will still be worthless Rats. Then the leaves will return and you will still be Rats."

That said, Hagan turns the podium over to Staub, who will inform the Rats about their class privileges.

"As Rats," Staub says, "your one and only privilege is to strain."

He then selects a volunteer to come up on stage and, with the help of some of his RDC members, demonstrate the VMI strain.

"The strain" is the position of attention exaggerated to the highest possible degree. Your chin cannot be tucked tightly enough into the cavity of your chest. Your

shoulders cannot be rolled back far enough. There is never enough arch in your back.
A Rat cannot do it right, so he needs help. Staub's assistants help the man chosen to
be a demonstrator.

They spread the fingers of their hands until they look like claws and then thrust them
close to the man's face until he has to push his chin in tighter to his neck — then tighter,
then even tighter — or find fingers in his eyes. They prod at his shoulders without ever
quite touching — until he rolls them back into a position that looks almost contorted.

"Back," they hiss, "get 'em back, Rat."

When the Rat demonstrator has it more or less right, the rest of the Rats get to try.
Staub and the other members of the RDC stand on the benches and use their hands like
claws, helping the Rats get it right.

"Do it, Rat. Do it. Get 'em back. Back."

It takes half an hour for the Rats to learn how to strain. They will have six months
to practice — until the leaves are on the trees again.

The Rats are herded from JM Hall to Cocke Hall, where the hops are held, including
the sacred Ring Figure. Tonight it is the scene of a different kind of dance.

Tonight, members of the first class will hold a sweat party for the Rats. The Rats
are lined up at one end of the gym, the dance floor, with intensely bright spot lights
shining on them so intensely they are completely blinded. The other end of the room
is dark. From a balcony, Hagan introduces the Rats to the first classmen who will, he
says, "Work you out."

The first classmen appear out of the darkness, advancing in line, as though in an
infantry assault. They come slowly at first, stomping a hard cadence out on the gym
floor, like the beat of a drum. When they are halfway across the floor, they break ranks

and rush the waiting Rats. Suddenly from the darkness they have descended—individually, in pairs, in gangs. The Rats are punished for being Rats. They must do pushups. Mountain climbers. Crunches. Run in place with their arms over their heads. The lights are intense and the noise worse, with Rats groaning and the first class-men bellowing. The room fills with the heat of straining bodies and the pungent stench of perspiration.

Several Rats drop out, or try to. But lying on the floor, exhausted, does not mean a man is left alone. He only gets it worse.

Then, after an hour, it is over . . . temporarily.

The Rats are marched up to the courtyard of New Barracks, where the seconds and thirds are waiting. The first class has generously given middle classmen permission to work out the new Rats.

Another sweat party follows, this one under a black, uncaring sky. Rats drop out and lean, exhausted, against the walls of the first stoop, unable to obey the screams to "Get up, get up and push, Rat."

Finally, an hour or so before BRC (Breakfast Roll Call), it is all over. The Rats are run back to their rooms and to the showers where, to their own surprise, some of them are laughing.

It isn't funny, when you think about it, one cadet says. But you can't think about it. And if you couldn't laugh, you'd go crazy. So you laugh. The ones who are already laughing will make it through, and the rest of them will learn. In this place a sense of humor is your life raft, your flak jacket, your Holy Bible. It's what gets you through.

A few Rats are still damp from the showers as the Corps forms for BRC and marches down to the mess hall for breakfast. The Ratline is in place; the Old Corps has returned; and another year has begun at the Virginia Military Institute.

The Code

The routine at VMI changes slowly and by small increments, when it changes at all. A graduate from fifty years ago would find the essentials of life in the barracks very familiar. While the world at large has changed extravagantly during his lifetime, VMI is very much the place it was when he was a cadet. It looks the same. The details of the day have the same feel. The cold early morning formations. Guard mount and the monotonous walking of your post around the sentinel box, rifle at right shoulder arms. Penalty tours. Room inspections. Formations and marching to meals. Friday afternoon parades.

To the cadets in the Old Corps—the first, second, and third classmen—the routine is comfortable and can be tedious, especially as the year wears on and winter settles over the valley. In their sameness, the days seem to stretch out bleakly into the future with no relief until the next vacation or the final release of graduation. No man has ever been through four years of VMI, no matter how much he came to love the place later, without feeling, at some time, that the place was slowly, remorselessly grinding him down. Nobody comes to VMI, or stays there, to have fun.

Least of all the Rats, for whom the routine has not yet become familiar and is anything but comforting.

A Rat's day begins early, with an alarm clock instead of a kick at the door. He crawls out of his hay at "Oh-dark-thirty," (about 5:30 AM, civilian time), gets himself dressed and goes down to the first stoop to wake his Dyke.

The Dyke system is one of those traditions that is baffling to outsiders, but obvious and essential to any VMI man. Even the word "dyke"— an early twentieth century corruption of the term "decked out," to imply dressed up — is confusing to strangers. At VMI it is an all-purpose term that, as the Rats already know, originally refers to uniforms. Used precisely, the "dyke" is the arrangement of crossed belts that are worn with a dress uniform. When you dress for a parade, you get "dyked-out." But the "dyke system" has nothing at all to do with uniforms and everything to do with VMI.

"Your Dyke is . . . well, I don't know exactly what he is," a Rat once said, trying to explain the mystery to a visitor. "Your Dyke is . . . well, he's your Dyke, you know. He's a first classman and he's like a big brother or an uncle or some older guy who's been around and knows things and can keep you from making all the mistakes he made. A good Dyke can get you through a lot."

If the first classman who is a mentor and advisor and confessor to a Rat is his Dyke, what does that make the Rat in this special, one-on-one relationship?

"I'm his Dyke," the Rat helpfully explains. In the Dyke system, the first classman and the Rat are each other's Dykes.

But if it is confusing for the outsider, it is clear to the cadets. And as the Rat learns about life at VMI, he learns just how important his Dyke can be to him. He wakes his Dyke up in the morning, rolls his hay and helps clean up his room before he leaves for class. And he does other errands and chores for his Dyke as well. All of this might not seem like such a bargain to outsiders, but for this extra work, the Rat gets support and advice and the occasional "suck it up" lecture that he needs. It is a relationship without formal rules, so it becomes what you make of it. You can have a Dyke who does just enough, merely goes through the motions, or you can have one who — usually because he had a good Dyke, himself — takes the job seriously and makes it his business to see that his Rat survives to become a good VMI man.

So it is common for a man's Dyke to become, later, best man at his wedding, the godfather — and sometimes, sadly, the guardian — of his children, a friend and something more, for life. "I've never been closer to anyone in the last thirty-five years," a distinguished VMI man once told a visitor, "than I've been to my Dyke." In a world that is just beginning to appreciate the virtues of "bonding" and "mentoring," VMI is in the unusual position of being right in step and, in fact, ahead of the society. (Though nobody at VMI would consider it in quite that sensitive a light.) The first class is responsible for the Rats, as a group (a Rat mass), and as individuals. The progress of the Rats — or the lack of it — reflects directly back on the first class and, in a way, each Rat mass is a mirror image of the first class that forms it. A tough, straight Rat mass usually means that the first class responsible for it had it hard as Rats. And the harder the class, the more crucial the advice and wisdom of the individual — the Dyke.

For a Rat, it is enough if your Dyke will just give you a place — his room — where you can be safe for a couple of hours every day. Nobody can come in and mess with you when you are in your Dyke's room, and a good Dyke will be generous with this

sanctuary. You can study or get a little sleep (on the floor, behind a desk, so you can't be seen through the window, from the stoop) between classes and avoid the various stairwells and passageways in the barracks—the Sally port, Pervert corner, Gold Coast, & Ghetto—which you would have to use to get to your own room, and where there are always a few upper classmen waiting to find something wrong with the way you are walking the Ratline—or something else—and to spend time amusing themselves by tormenting you. Your Dyke can give you a measure of relief from this as well as advice that will help you keep out of your own way.

You learn the routine from being told about it by your Dyke, and you learn it through doing, by sheer repetition. You are told to walk the Ratline in barracks and to salute the statue of Stonewall Jackson whenever you exit Jackson arch. For the first few times, a Rat will have to remind himself. If he forgets, he can be sure that there will be an upper classman close by to remind him.

"Drop, Rat and give me ten. You don't have to salute, huh? What makes you so special? Every other Rat who ever came through here had to salute, but you don't have to, huh?"

Above:

Rats and dykes on the stoop.

Following pages:

Dyking out. The final steps. Brian Bagwan's dyke, with pins in teeth, gives him the final wrap.

Above:

Flamers without peer, the
Four Horsemen of
'96–'97: Pridgen, Himel,
Smith, & Zoffuto.

Within a few days, you render that salute without thinking about it.

You learn how to roll your hay. How to clean your room. Spit shine shoes. Polish brass. Break starch. Clean your rifle. Recite your general orders, your chain of command, the name of the president of the Honor Court, and the other information in your Rat Bible for which you are responsible.

But all that is merely the official learning process. There is a lot more to learn that is not, necessarily, in *The Bullet* or any other book.

You learn a language, for one thing. Some of it official and some not. Every Rat learns, very quickly, what it means to be "boned." He learns that if it happens to him often enough, he will be out on the bricks—Tuesday, Thursday, and Saturday—walking PTs. If he can avoid getting boned for a full four week demerit period—which is good—it will be called "running a period."

The Rats learn quickly who the Rat Daddies are: the upper classmen who, for reasons known only to them, take pity on Rats, treat them with kindness, and even help them out of the clutches of the flamers, who tend to the opposite extreme and believe that no Rat can possibly suffer enough.

The Rats learn about their own, too. The learn who the BRFs are. And the "permit worms," "gim riders," and "smack Rats." A bond grows among the Rats, but some are never fully admitted to the brotherhood.

You learn how the day runs. From BRC to DRC to SRC; and about CQ, CCQ, and CQRB. Before long, it all makes as much sense to the Rats as it does to the upper classmen, who schedule their lives according to these acronyms.

Rats learn what it means to "run the block," though they don't (yet) do much of it themselves and probably do not know that the term has its origins, like so much around VMI, in the Civil War. Running the block comes from running the blockade of Union ships that kept cargo vessels from reaching Southern ports. Some such evasions were successful, just as some VMI cadets manage to leave Post, without authorization, for the night life of Lexington and places beyond, without getting caught.

The language becomes as familiar as the routine. You speak nonchalantly of the sinks (the level a half-flight below the first stoop and the courtyard, where some first classmen live, as well as cadets who have returned for a fifth year to finish required courses), and you know about the OD and that he walks around jangling a heavy ring of keys to alert anyone who is in violation of any of the myriad VMI rules because it is his duty to put any violator he catches on the bone sheet.

You learn about some things that everyone knows but that are nowhere officially acknowledged. George C. Marshall, winner of the Nobel Peace Prize, General of the Army, architect of the Allied victory in World War II, is easily the most distinguished of all VMI graduates. During his entire Army career, he suffered from a trick knee that was the result of a session he was put through as a Rat. Marshall was forced to squat over a bayonet and, perhaps because he was still recovering from an illness or possibly because things went a little far, he passed out. He barely missed impaling himself on the bayonet. In the process he permanently injured his knee.

Marshall refused to report the names of the men who had made him squat over the point of that bayonet. He was intensely loyal to VMI—then and all the rest of his life.

Life at VMI is ruled by codes within codes. What seems alien in those first hours of Cadre Week becomes not just understandable, but something to embrace. An upper classman will work a Rat out—and go beyond what is strictly authorized—to show him he's willing to risk punishment from the administration if he is caught. And the Rat will do the workout and not report it to show that he can take it.

Most Rats learn soon enough about the RDC, the Rat Disciplinary Committee. The way you learn is when you are informed, through a simple 3 x 5 card delivered to your room, that you have been summoned by the RDC to answer charges, that night after taps. It is called an invitation, but you cannot send regrets.

After taps, in your BDUs, you report at the stairwell next to Jackson Arch that leads down to the sinks . The members of the RDC are there, waiting for you. They are not happy.

There might be a dozen Rats and they will be led, single file, down past the first class rooms in the sinks, deeper below Old Barracks, into the rooms where the steam pipes pass heat up into the barracks. The experience is very much like passing down into a dungeon.

The Rats are assembled in one small, hot room where the lights are bright and the members of the RDC make sure that you are kept busy doing pushups and mountain climbers and other familiar exercises while you wait to be called into the next room, where court is in session.

That room is dark. The walls are painted black and sweat from the heat of the pipes. A single, intense light is focused on the accused.

"Rat _____," a voice comes at you from the dark, "you have been accused of failing to shower for twenty-four hours, and wearing BDUs that stink. How do you answer the charges?"

"Correct, Sir."

A strobe begins flashing, and suddenly there are three or four faces close to yours.

"Strain, Rat. You'd better strain. God, I can smell you in here. Don't you care about your Brother Rats? Do you want them to have to smell you?"

"No Sir."

"Get down, Rat."

"Get up, Rat."

"Hands over your head, Rat."

"Run."

The Rat begins running, frantically, in place. Churning his legs, bringing his knees up high. A speaker blasts some kind of loud noise that might be music — heavy metal, they would call it out in the civilian world, but down here it is just noise. And someone begins beating on the wall with a metal dust pan. The sound is utterly disorienting. The voices scream at you from the darkness to run, push, get up, get down. It might

Above:

RDC president Jeffrey *Staub interrogates a Rat.*

as well be August on the parade ground, the way you're sweating. You feel trapped in that small, hot, dark, noisy room — crowded with all those men whose faces pop in and out of focus with the blinking of the strobe. The effect is claustrophobically intense, sensory overload.

When you stop running, the voice comes out of the darkness.

"Rat, you have been found guilty. You will do five Rat penalty tours. Do you understand."

"Yes Sir."

"And you will shower every day, do you understand?"

"Yes Sir."

When you get back to your room, drenched with sweat and with your ears still ringing, your BRs inevitably want to know how it went.

And you tell them — five PTs and a warning not to miss another shower.

"Not too terrible." You tell the whole story and you laugh. Or try to, anyway. You are learning just how much you can take, which is one part of the code.

If the RDC's job is to enforce the disciplinary code of day-to-day life, it has no jurisdiction over more serious offenses. Of all the written and unwritten codes, and codes within codes, that regulate life at VMI, it is the Honor Code that exemplifies what VMI really stands for. A cadet will not entirely understand the truth of this until his first "drum out" drives the point home.

Within a few days of matriculation, the entire Rat class meets with the president of the Honor Court for a briefing that — difficult as it might be to imagine — is even more sobering than anything that has gone before.

The 1996–97 Honor Court president is a first classman named Joe Steele and the name fits. He is a formidable looking man: stern and uncompromising, just like the code his classmates have entrusted him to uphold.

"Rats," he begins, "as students of the twenty-first century, you will soon find that society's path to success is littered with the selfish ideals of instant gratification and personal gain. Rats, VMI will not accept the faults of the world in which you live as an excuse for dishonorable conduct. Instead, VMI will consistently expect you to place honor above self in all that you do. There is no such thing as a viable alternative or reasonable compromise when faced with the decision to act honorably."

Steele has the complete and utter attention of the Rat mass in JM Hall as he continues.

"Rats, the Honor System at VMI derives its authority from the Honor Code. The Honor Code is not difficult to follow or clouded by unclear distinctions. It simply states, A CADET WILL NEITHER LIE, CHEAT, STEAL, NOR TOLERATE THOSE WHO DO . . . If you choose to violate the Honor Code, I can assure you that this Court will exhaust itself in a calculated effort to remove you from our presence. Consider yourself warned . . . . The Court will insure that the accused is given ample time to prepare his defense. . . . but only two verdicts are possible. A cadet will either be found guilty or not guilty. . . . There is no other option. If a cadet is found not guilty he is completely exonerated of all charges and bears no stigma. However, if a cadet is found guilty, he is immediately dismissed from the Institute in the usual manner."

The meaning of this phrase — "the usual manner" — is left unspoken. The Rats, who return to Old Barracks both deeply impressed and very curious, will learn soon enough.

It is long after taps — 0330 hours — and the stoops are still except for the footsteps and jingling keys of the OD and the TAC making their rounds. You are in your hay, trying to get some sleep before it all starts again, when a steady, ominous roll of snare drums begins down in the courtyard and somebody abruptly opens the door just as the sound of a bass drum, punctuating the roll of the snares, echoes through the courtyard.

"Get out on the stoop," a voice commands, "the Honor Court has met."

Shivering and half awake and, in the case of the Rats, not knowing what to expect, cadets gather on the stoops, a thousand of them in the darkness, around a dark courtyard. All the electricity inside Barracks is turned off and it is totally dark except for the weak light provided by the stars and a late moon in the dark sky and by the orange glow of a few cigarettes around the stoops.

The drum roll dies. For a moment there is a vast, early morning silence. Then the voice of the president of the Honor Court, from inside Jackson Arch.

"Court, atten . . . hut."

"Forward . . . march."

With the president out front, the entire membership of the Honor Court marches into the courtyard, dressed in coatees.

"Court . . . halt."

The president of the Court then marches out to the sentinel box and makes his speech as he circles it:

"Tonight, the Honor Court has met and after a trial Cadet fourth classman _____ has been found guilty on two counts of making false official statements. He has placed personal gain above personal honor and has left the institute in shame. His name will never be used within the four walls of barracks . . . AGAIN."

Before the last words have died on the air, the cadets on the stoop have turned away, as though from the offender himself, and are returning to their rooms. A few are muttering.

"Jesus."

"Oh man."

"You believe that dumb bastard? Risk it all . . . for that."

What "that" is, seems unimportant to them. Nothing, large or small, could be worth this disgrace. In the old days, the guilty man had to stand out there in front of the Corps, in shame, and when the president had finished his speech he was led out of barracks and sent away for good. The modern drum out seems only a little less humiliating.

That was my first drum out," one Rat says later, "and I didn't go back to sleep all night."

"You never do," a first classman said. "You never do."

The next day, and for a few days after that, the Rats talk among themselves about the case, even as they are careful not to use the name of the guilty man. Everyone seems to know that the cadet in question had signed a statement certifying that he had done the five pullups required to meet the Institute's physical fitness standards. He had not done the pullups and one of his BRs, who had been there when he failed to do so, had reported the violation to the Honor Court, as he was required to do. Not to have made the report would, itself, have been a violation. The code is absolutely clear on this point.

So the man was "rolled" over a few simple exercises. If he had told the truth—that he could not do the pullups—he would have been required to do extra PT until he could pass the requirement. It is easy to imagine how typical college students today would view the ingredients and end result of such an incident: the pullups requirement, the obligation to report a fellow student, the punishment. "Man," you can imagine one of them saying in disbelief, "you mean that you messed up a guy's whole life over a few lousy pullups?"

To someone who is part of the brotherhood and bound by all the codes however, this is coming at it from an entirely wrong direction.

"Can you believe that anyone would do something like that to himself, just to keep from doing a little extra PT?" one of the banished man's former BRs says. The content and tone of his question accurately reflects the view inside the Corps.

The difference is far more fundamental than a simple difference in perspective, and is one more measure of how far the paths of the men in the barracks have diverged from those of their old friends and associates outside. Cheating is no big deal at most colleges. Honor is considered antique. Students out there cannot believe that a code of behavior should be taken more seriously than a student's self interest. Cadets inside the brotherhood cannot believe that a student would allow his self interest to take precedence over the code governing his fellow students.

"There isn't anything at VMI that is taken more seriously," Cadet Joe Steele says of the Honor System. "When the President of the first class, or the head of the RDC, speaks to the rest of the class, some of the guys will boo him or heckle him, you know, just clowning around, or even seriously. But when I get up to speak, it's different. Everybody pays attention. Not because of me, but for what I represent."

The Honor Court meets in secret. The rooms where it meets are secure and as formally appointed as any courtroom. Witnesses do not tell their roommates where they have been when they come back to the barracks after testifying. Everything about the Honor Code is approached with utter seriousness.

True, the hell raiser has a certain place at VMI. But not the man who lies, cheats, steals or tolerates those who do. You will report your roommate, your best friend, your Brother Rat, your Dyke . . . anyone. And the system, which consists of cadets who prosecute and who rule on the evidence, can return only one of two verdicts. Either you are cleared and your honor is unstained and intact. Or you are guilty and the drums will roll and you will be gone for good, on a "bongo furlough."

In a relativistic world, life at VMI is still run according to absolutes. From the moment he arrives, the new VMI man feels a distance growing between himself and his old life and friends. They have hair and he does not. They wear the clothes they want to wear; he wears a uniform. They organize their lives according to their own needs; his day is so rigorously scheduled that he marches to meals. To them, right and wrong are different shades of the same color—gray—while he lives according to the inflexible standards of the Honor Code. There is nothing like a drum out to make a VMI man aware of the difference between his world and the one he's left behind.

Following pages:

Life in steel and concrete.

Chemistry, calculus, and history: as stressful as the Ratline.

On the first three inches of your chair: "Enjoy your meal, Rat."

Bathrobe dyke.

Ten minutes before parade formation.

Dyking out for Friday parade.

Polishing brass. An endless chore.

Ready for inspection: racks folded, hays rolled.

Polishing shoes to a spit shine.

First Class Privates' Belt and Buckle. The buckle is cast from a mold made from a New Market cartridge box. The dent above the letter "M" is not—as legend sometimes has it—from a bullet at New Market, but from a flaw in the mold, left there to distinguish replicas from the original.

First class president Addison Hagan attends to details.

Guard mount.

The OD keeps his keys jingling as a warning.

Stepping off for parade.

The Barracks

❖

Ring Figure and the VMI Spirit

❖

he first three months of the VMI year move briskly. There are football games and visitors. The old grads return for Founders' Day and Homecoming and on other weekends, simply to make the trip in the fall when the Institute feels especially vital. Loyalty in VMI grads seems to grow almost in proportion to the time they've been gone. And there is no more loyal group of alumni at any school, anywhere. They are the glue that holds the Institute together. The VMI alumni give back generously: The Institute is by far the most heavily-endowed public school, per capita, in the nation. The alumni serve on the VMI Foundation, on the Board of Visitors, at alumni chapters around the country.

VMI's alumni are evidence that life in the barracks and the discipline of the Ratline serves some larger purpose than discipline for its own sake. Any outsider who wonders why, in the late twentieth century, any young person would willingly put himself through this kind of tough four-year regimen, need only look to the many graduates who feel a profound, enduring loyalty to the place. And it is not simple coincidence that so many of them have done well in life.

The military accomplishments of VMI graduates are easy enough to account for. Yet, even if most of the men who return on these Fall weekends have served in the armed forces, few are active duty officers. They are civilians who have made their mark across many fields. The executives among them have been chairmen of Fortune 500 companies or run large humanitarian organizations. The lawyers among them include a former President of the Virginia Bar. Living graduates have served in the U.S. Senate, coached NFL Super Bowl teams, written bestselling novels, and starred in top television shows. They are businessmen, financiers and, especially, engineers with their own companies—sometimes it seems as if they have built most of the roads and bridges in the state of Virginia.

It has always been the goal of VMI to train citizen-soldiers. The graduates who give so lavishly to the school, who return to the Post to once again walk the barracks with their families, are the best possible argument for the wisdom of the VMI system. Their affection for the Institute is on display most conspicuously during those fall weekends when the old Brother Rats come back by the hundreds and gather by class to march down the parade ground after the Corps has passed in review. If the old grads' ranks are raggedly aligned and they are mostly out of step, carrying umbrellas instead of rifles, they are enthusiastic, especially when they make it back into the courtyard of the barracks and they give the Old Yells with one of them standing on the sentinel box leading the rest of them on.

Alumni weekend

❖

The young men who are still cadets draw from the enthusiasm and spirit of the old grads. Even the Rats feel it. The walls of the barracks seem to quake with the cheering and the pounding of the drums and the thudding of rifle butts on the concrete floors of the stoops. Banners wave in the crisp fall air as the voices of three generations of VMI men fill the courtyard and spill out over the walls so loudly you can hear the roar up in Lexington.

RAH VIRGINIA MIL!

RAH, RAH, RAH!

RI-RI, VMI

'57, '57, '57

The sound of the cheers rocks the barracks and seems to echo long after the courtyard is cleared and the Corps has formed up to march down to the stadium for the game.

The parents of a Rat, visiting the school on one of those fall weekends, can be in for a shock. If they have not seen their son since matriculation, they will be surprised by the way he looks. The hair, of course, will take some getting used to, as will the physical changes. The Rats who arrived plump and out of shape will have lost weight and gotten harder. The men who were skinny two months ago will have put on muscle. Pushups are great for changing a physique.

Then there's the way the young man looks in uniform. It takes time to learn how to wear a uniform (which is why most movie actors look so unconvincing in military roles), and after a couple of months, a Rat has finally got the look. He has been issued his gray blouse, the style of which goes back to the nineteenth century and the founding of VMI. The uniform is made of pure 23-ounce wool and tailored by a firm in New York, and before a Rat can wear it right, his Dyke needs to show him how. It actually takes practice to keep the gray blouse from bunching up so that it maintains a smooth, seamless fit. You cannot look at a young man wearing a uniform that way and think of him, any longer, as your baby boy.

"I cried more when I saw him the first time, like that," one mother said to a VMI visitor, "than I did when we left him here. He was so . . . different."

Parents, siblings, friends—they all notice how much you have changed in such a short time. And what has changed perhaps most is something that they can't see at all. Happy as you are to see the old faces, you feel a distance from them . . . no loss of love, just a distinct separation. They are still your family and your friends, but you don't share with them what you share with the men you now think of as your Brother Rats.

The bond that has been forming is slowly being forged into something stronger than you could once have imagined. It now seems intensely important that every one of you make it, that you all come through together. You have learned to do a lot together, already, and you are holding up to the worst the flamers can dish out. You are starting to get a feel for the place, a sense that you can handle it. And if some of you are a little uncertain, a little weaker than the others, then the strong ones will pull you through. That's the way it works. If you are having trouble, your Brother Rats pull you through. You don't have to make it alone and, in fact, you can't.

Still, once Cadre Week is over and the people who obviously did not belong have gone, you never really know for sure which of your Brother Rats are brooding deeply on the possibility of quitting. You share everything and you talk about everything . . . except that. Because you know if you talk about quitting, your Brother Rats will be all over you, working hard to talk you out of it.

The more seriously a man thinks about quitting, the less likely he is to talk about it. "We have the maggot of the Corps, right here in our room," a cheerful Rat told a visitor one day in the fall of '96. "This guy has a hard time with everything. He learns slow and he's physically weak.

"It took him two days to learn how to do the rifle movements for 'inspection arms' and he still couldn't do it right because he wasn't strong enough to get the bolt back without jamming the rifle against his body. And he has an expression on his face, that he can't help, that makes it look like he's kind of laughing when he's really scared. So the flamers get on him and they think he doesn't take them seriously, that he's smirking. They do all kinds of things to him, to make him doubt himself. They'll make him stand in front of a mirror and flame himself; you know, scream at himself that he is a worthless piece of crap and that he doesn't belong at VMI. They're on him like white on rice.

"But we're going to get him through."

The Rat who was talking was one of the real performers in his class. You could look at him and see that he had it. He looked good in his uniform. He had arms like fence posts, so he could handle the pushups. He could march and do the manual of arms before any of the other Rats in his company because he had been to a military boarding school but had the sense to keep quiet about it. He was even good at his class work. First marking period, he was on the dean's list. He had never been invited to one of the RDC sessions. His BRs looked up to him. He was Cadre material and, plainly, he would not merely make it, he would excel. And he had made it his mission—along with his other roommates—to get "the maggot of the Corps" through the Ratline.

"I'll be all right," said "the maggot" to the visitor. "It's hard, but I'll be all right." He had nervous hands and he looked at the ground when he talked. He still did not look right in a uniform. It hung limply on his frame. His shoes, even when he had just finished working on them, did not have that gleam. Neither did his eyes.

But he kept up a good front for his roommates, telling a couple of them from out West that he would fix them up for dates with girls he knew from his hometown in Virginia. And he kept flaming himself in the mirror, working on the manual of arms, knocking out pushups, getting called down to RDC, and generally suffering the fate of a Rat who has been picked out for special attention.

On a weekend in early November, the man's mother came to visit. He went out to dinner with her on Saturday night and did not make it back for taps. He was reported absent at bed check, and again in the morning at BRC.

His roommates never saw him again.

"We never had a clue," the man who had vowed to get him through said. "Right up until the end, he was still talking about fixing us up with dates, still smiling when he told us what the flamers had made him do, still needing help with his uniform before Friday afternoon parade. We boxed his stuff up. Never heard a word from him."

Most cadets, though, survive the fall because of those weekends when there are visitors and—a gift from on high—when the football team wins and the first class president asks the Superintendent to grant special leave privileges and suspends the Ratline. A victory against arch rival The Citadel, like the one in the Oyster Bowl of 1996, when Tommy Haskins scored a touchdown in the second overtime, is a fine thing by itself, but it is ten times sweeter for the taste of freedom that comes with it: the freedom to walk up a flight of stairs and to stroll along the stoop, making lazy turns and letting your arms swing loosely at your sides.

Monday morning comes, of course. And the fall days turn colder and shorter so the Friday afternoon parades are held as the sun's last light fades over a chilly parade ground and the Corps marches in overcoats with red-lined capes. On one of those Friday afternoons, when the sun is low and House Mountain glows with a sort of golden hue and the afternoon air is cold, almost freezing, the Corps forms up in the courtyard. There are the usual officers in uniform, including the Superintendent, out on the parade ground to review the Corps. Also a few visitors. Some parents and girlfriends who have come for the weekend, as well as some tourists and locals who simply enjoy watching a good military parade. By this part of the year, the Corps is capable of putting on a parade as precise and stirring as any you will see in America—and that includes West Point or Annapolis.

The band is a big part of what makes a VMI parade. The band has been working on both its music and its marching since Cadre Week. They have drilled and played hard, working two afternoons during the week and for an hour every Saturday, training as diligently as any athletes so they will march and play with the crisp authority you expect from a military band.

John Brodie is band director. He is a colonel in the Virginia Militia, but more to the point, he is a former enlisted Marine who went though boot camp where he was honor man in his class. As a musician, he could have skipped that part of the Marine

Corps experience but he did it because, he says, "It seemed like if you were going to wear a Marine Corps uniform, then you should go through the Marine Corps experience." He has the right kind of attitude for VMI, where playing in the band doesn't really buy you out of much. It isn't like a sports permit. A Rat in the band gets the full Ratline experience, just like Brodie got the full Marine Corps experience.

The first VMI musicians, in 1839, were two slaves who played the fife and drum. For the next one hundred years, music for parades was provided by hired musicians who were not cadets. These VMI bands resembled those at the service academies today, which are made up, not of cadets or midshipmen, but active-duty, enlisted personnel. The first VMI cadet band, in 1947, consisted of twenty-two cadets. Fifty years later, that number had grown to 115. Most of them come to VMI with some musical background. But Brodie still has his work cut out: "I have made a lot of rock guitarists into trombone or trumpet players."

There are benefits to being in the band, even if it does not get you out of the Ratline or the normal military duties that football players and other varsity athletes can escape. For one thing, there are trips. The band has led the St. Patrick's Day parade in New York, and until 1992, when the VMI court case was being prominently reported in the media, it routinely marched in Washington at the Inauguration. In 1997 the band went to New Orleans for Mardi Gras, where it was judged "best band" in one of the famous parades down St. Charles Street. In 1988, the band marched in Paris as part of the bicentennial celebration of the French Revolution.

At home on a cold, clear Friday afternoon, as the band comes through Jackson Arch with the drums echoing against stone until spectators can feel it in their bones, the sound is deep and stirring; the sound of troops on parade. They play the marches every VMI man remembers. "The Bonnie Blue Flag." "Shenandoah." There was a time when they would have played "Dixie," but that tradition ended after a dignified protest in 1969 from black cadets.

Once the band has cleared the arch, the rest of the Corps follows, all nine companies, from Alpha—where the basketball players can be found—down through "F-troop" and on to India Company. India Company is composed of the shortest cadets in the Corps—many of them from Asian nations, whose Armies and Navies they will one day command. For the first few parades of the year, the Rats march in a separate formation behind the rest of the Corps. It is a day of great pride when they are integrated into their companies with the rest of the Corps.

By November, even the Rats have been at it long enough to know how to do it right. A visitor standing in the courtyard five minutes before parade formation will wonder if his watch is keeping good time. The courtyard will be quiet, still, and virtually empty. As the time draws down, and the PA system announces the minutes left until formation, doors along the stoop open and men appear, dressed and ready, sauntering down the steps and into the courtyard. As time gets shorter, the cadets move with more haste, until the last few are hustling to make it before the last bugle note. "Hold it," the last couple of men say and the bugler holds the note until they are in place. The cadets know how to squeeze every second out of the countdown. When the moment comes, they will be formed up, in the courtyard, banging rifle butts on the concrete and getting pumped up for the parade.

Once the weather turns cold, cadets will wear overcoats with red-lined capes that were originally added to the uniform so that a cadet who was running the block could

Following pages:

Forming up for New Market parade in full dyke, rain or shine.

Third classmen two minutes before forming up: strictly routine.

The cadet band, on parade, entering the arch before adjutant's call.

Officer's belt brass.

Dress and cover. Dress and cover."

Bring your battalions to parade rest."

Regimental staff taking the review.

Full Dress Parade

be picked out of a crowd of civilians. But on a cold Friday, with the sun going down and snow on the ground, the capes add a touch of splendor to an otherwise drab and monochromatic scene. Against the bare trees and the flat mustard walls of the Institute, the red capes look especially dramatic. The cadets march out onto the parade ground with a crisp cadence and precise movements. No spectator watching this parade feels he is looking at college boys playing soldier; this is the real thing.

The Rats feel this especially. In the weeks since they assembled on this same parade ground wearing athletic shoes and BDUs and fumbled through the movements that the exasperated Cadre tried to teach them, they have gotten first better, then good, and finally expert at the intricacies of elementary close order drill. Drill of this kind is a fundamental skill that has its own learning curve, and as the Rats mastered the movements, their confidence and cohesion increased. Now they not only march in step and in straight ranks with rifles in alignment, but their uniforms fit perfectly.

Back in their rooms on the fourth stoop they have looked at themselves and each other and corrected the small flaws—the twisted dykes and curled collars and half buttoned buttons—before moving down the stairs to form up. They are beginning to savor the taste of confidence.

The distant hills turn purple, then dark as the Corps passes in review, and the cadets feel the sweet, shared emotion of soldiers on parade; that old, old sense of belonging to something larger than themselves, the pride of being part of a unit that can take the routine business of marching in formation and turn it into something that makes the heart of every man in ranks beat a little faster.

The leaves have fallen and the Rats are still in the Ratline. The class room work begins to grind. "Thermal godammics," "orgasmic chemistry," "diffy calc" and the other killer courses are threatening to weed out third classmen who thought they had it made after surviving the Ratline. The engines of discipline are cracking down on cadets caught running the block and coming back Saturday night on too much beer. An escapade like that gets you an automatic "number one": four months' confinement (until after Christmas), loss of rank if you have any, a pile of demerits, and many hours on the bricks with the "cross country hiking and gun club." You see these men out walking PTs, some with a faint outline on their sleeves where the stripes used to be. It is never easy, even now, during a generally agreeable part of the year. Any letup is strictly temporary. After a good football win, for a few hours. Then back to the grind.

For the second class, there is one special weekend during this season that represents much more than mere relief from routine. It is the high point in every cadet's VMI life to this time, an event that matches anything except, possibly, graduation.

Ring Figure is, strictly speaking, just a dance. A glorified junior prom. But this, as any VMI man can tell you, is like saying that the Super Bowl is just another football game.

The actual formal dance is ceremonially impressive. The achingly slow introduction of each second classman, the walk through the giant replica of the ring which has been around for years and is touched up every year for this occasion, the formal presentation of the ring by a radiant young woman in a ball gown, the forming of the class number by the men and their dates... all this lends the celebration a particular solemnity. Many of the cadets have parents there, watching proudly, which only adds to the significance. But all this would amount to just another hop—nice but no great big deal—without the object around which the ritual revolves, which is also the object of every second classman's utmost affection: the ring.

It is difficult to exaggerate just how much that ring means to the men who are about to wear it for the first time. The class ring has been around since 1848, but the tradition has grown, along with the size of the ring itself, until it reached its present, almost mythic import. Formal, annual presentation of rings to second classmen came along in 1908. The Ring Figure dance in 1928. As the tradition grew, so did the importance of the ring itself. Cadets who have accidentally left rings behind at fraternity houses at W & L or Tech have been known to go back for them with a platoon of their BRs, dressed in gray blouse and ready for combat.

At one level the ring is simple adornment. VMI cadets wear austere uniforms and no jewelry. They keep their hair cut short and their faces shaved. They have smooth-toed, black shoes on their feet. There is nothing gaudy in their dress and grooming. So that big ring soothes a lot of latent, frustrated vanity.

Such a superficial explanation does not go near deep enough, however. For many VMI men, there is something almost mystical about the ring. First, the ring is a symbol. All of the small icons that have been worked into the design and etched into the gold are symbols of what the class that wears it has experienced, and what the Institute itself has gone through during the time the class has been there. In the case of the class of '98, there is a small legal scroll etched into the ring to symbolize the long and frustrating legal case that ended before the Supreme Court. The ring, then, is a kind of coded history of the life of the class.

Second, there is the sense of belonging that comes when a second classman's date puts the heavy ring onto his finger. He is now part of the brotherhood. Wearing the ring means that he has moved beyond a kind of probationary condition. His status has changed profoundly.

Third, the ring seems to have a life of its own. Men find that while it is possible to lose a ring even while still cadets, the rings have a way of almost always being found. You get in a snowball fight, for instance, the way one cadet did, and your ring comes off and is buried under three feet of snow. You dig frantically but you can't find it. And when the thaw comes, the ring isn't where it is supposed to be. Then, just about the time you've given up, decided that somebody (not a VMI man) found it and pawned it, a cadet walks into your room with the ring in hand and the story about how he found it. There are several famous stories about VMI rings that turned up years after they were lost in combat, or taken from the finger of a man killed in action, stories that go back to the Philippines in World War II, and to Korea, and Vietnam.

All of this lends a particular significance to the festivities surrounding the weekend that is Ring Figure: the formal dance; the class parties, which run late and wild; the extra intoxication that comes when you look down at your hand and see that huge, ornate ring. This is a celebration like no other celebration in a man's time at VMI. The first class clears out and the seconds run the Post. They have their rings now, and when a man looks down at his hand on Ring Figure Weekend and dreamily admires the big hunk of engraved gold resting there on his finger, what he feels is glory.

In November, after Ring Figure and before Thanksgiving furlough, restlessness becomes the prevailing mood in barracks—especially among the Rats. It has been a long time since matriculation and Cadre Week, and there is a kind of palpable tension in the air.

The flamers bring it on harder than ever and the Rats are feeling stirrings of that cohesion and unity that is the point of the Ratline. They are still not a class—still merely a Rat mass—but they are not a bunch of frightened, isolated individuals, either. Leaders have emerged among the Rats who are feeling frisky and rebellious, and eager to make a statement. The boldest among them push the rules and get called down for RDC, and inevitably the pent-up feelings of the Rats finds a release.

Some Rat suggests making a bonfire in the shape of their Dykes' class number out of their Rat bibles and burning it into the surface of the courtyard in New Barracks. They do it one night at taps, and after they do, they pay with an especially grueling sweat party. Still, they feel damned good about it.

Then, on another night, the entire Rat mass charges out of barracks and swarms the 105 howitzer on the parade ground. The wheels of the cannon are locked in place, but the shouting, struggling Rats still manage to push the gun across the parade ground, with the wheels digging furrows into the earth until they have placed the cannon squarely in front of the Commandant's quarters. The Rat mass is still not satisfied and moves, yelling incomprehensibly all the way down to the mess hall, where it proceeds to take out its frustrations, and demonstrate its unity, by smashing dishes.

The outburst is spontaneous, but hardly pointless. The Rats are not just a bunch of college boys who have played a fraternity prank and then gone skulking back to their dormitory rooms feeling slightly ashamed of themselves. This was something different. This was a statement. They may have been stripped of their individuality, but they have now come together as a group, and they are strong and unified. They have a new kind of confidence, and if they have to face the wrath of the Commandant and the firsts (who will lose some of their privileges until the Rats find a way to pay for the several thousand dollars of damages) well, bring it on. They can take it. All of it. And more.

Thanksgiving furlough comes at last. It is a temptation for the Rats who have been wavering. They have been able to manage in the barracks, with the support of their Brother Rats and because, as long as you are physically there at the I, quitting is not easy. You have to explain yourself and justify yourself to a lot of people. But when you get home, with your family and your old friends, you don't have to explain yourself to anyone. Especially when you're out with your old friends drinking beer, and they can't seem to understand why anyone would put up with it for a single day. Rats rediscover the satisfaction of sleeping late and going through a day without walking an imaginary line at attention, running up and down stairs, saluting an old bronze statue, and dropping for pushups when somebody who is only a couple of years older than you starts screaming. Going back becomes something to be dreaded.

Still, in '96 all the Rats returned to face a long three weeks until Christmas furlough. Back into the Ratline, after a brief taste of freedom. Back to waiting in the cold outside their Dykes' rooms, noses pressed to the wall until it was time to enter and begin another day of harassment and the peculiar, unending stresses of the Ratline.

There is one moment just before Christmas when the Corps feels keenly the pride of a cohesive military unit. At sunset, the Corps marches up the main street of Lexington. This is the only occasion when it parades through town. The music makes the men march tall for the admiring civilians on the sidewalks. It is a good parade and a good feeling, and knowing that there will now be almost a month at home, away from the Institute, makes it that much better.

Opposite:

The ring is a kind of coded history of the life of the class.

Following pages:

The second class in JM Hall, prior to receiving their rings.

The finest of all the hops: Ring Figure.

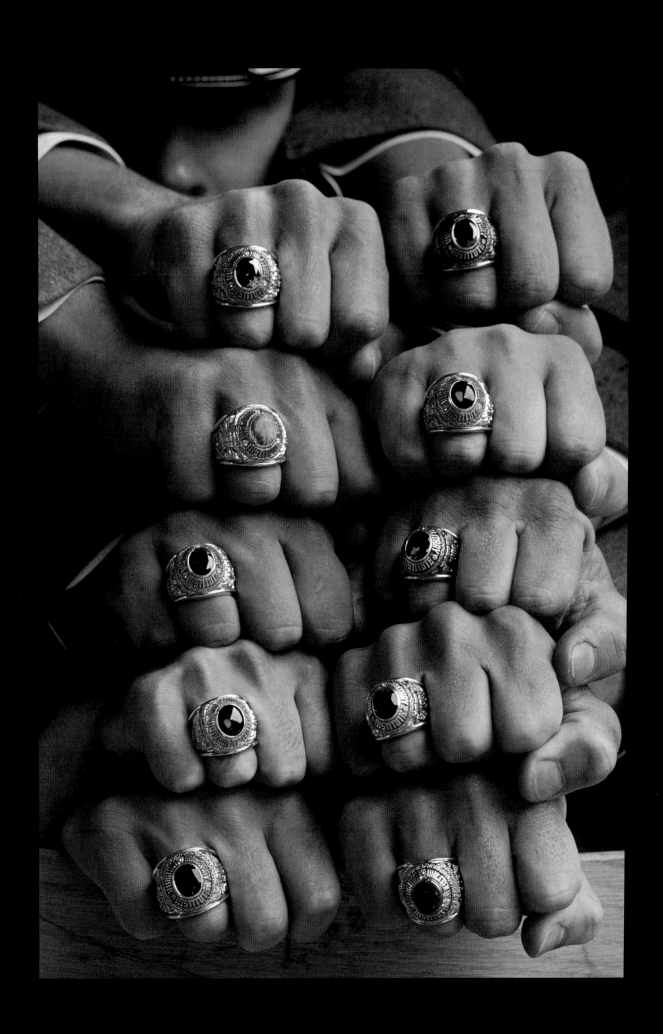

RESERVED
SECOND CLASS
SEATING

RESERVED
SECOND CLASS
SEATING

RESERVED
SECOND CLASS
SEATING

The Dark Ages

❖

Throughout Rats who return after Christmas furlough (twelve do not) will make it. About fifteen percent of those who matriculated are no longer at the I. They have quit (a few have been rolled), and they are missed but not mourned on the fourth stoop, where those who remain are determined to become part of the next class at VMI. It isn't over. Not yet and not by a long way. But the soft, marginal men who shouldn't have been here in the first place, who didn't really want it, are gone and those who remain are, more than ever, a hard core.

In the eyes of the first class, however, they still have a long way to go. There is a hard core within the first class too. And they inevitably believe that the Rats still have a lot to prove, and that the administration is doing what it can to make sure that they will never have to prove it. Part of the ever-present tension in the air at VMI stems from the more or less constant belief that the administration is trying to subvert the authority of the first class. There is grumbling, down in the sinks, about how the Rats are being babied, about how some first classmen are being singled out for going too far. The grumbling is at its most intense after Christmas, when everyone is getting tired of the pressure. The Ratline is hard on everyone. Even on the cadets who fervently believe that it is their duty to enforce discipline, and who are determined not to let up just because the end is, if only dimly, in sight.

"I got hauled up for unauthorized workout. Had a Rat in my room, doing pushups. You believe that. And I'll probably lose my stripes."

"The Rats know, man. They know. Just look at them, walking around. They're barely straining. They think they've got it made."

"Why not? With the way things are right now."

There is a certain amount of mutinous talk in the air. If things keep going this way, with the administration undercutting the first class, then maybe it is time for a step off.

It is usually just talk. The kind of grumbling that is typical and healthy in any military environment. But there have been rebellions at VMI. The first occurred in 1851, when the entire first class was dismissed, then reinstated but confined to Post until graduation. The rebellion was sparked by the refusal of the administration to extend some special leave privileges, but the cause of such episodes at VMI is almost always a pretext. Tension between the cadets—especially the first class—and the administration is inevitable and almost organic.

The rebellions have continued into the present era, the most celebrated occurring in 1951 when cadets, frustrated again over the curtailment of free time, broke windows, flooded rooms, and generally went on a rampage. As punishment, the entire corps was formed up at JM Hall, dressed down, and sent on a forced march in full field gear from 0100 to 0400. The episode was widely reported in the press as "The Rebellion of the Virginia Cadets."

The most common form of rebellion, to protest what first classmen consider interference by the administration with their authority over the Rats, is suspending the Ratline. It too is nothing new. It happened in 1934, and again, most famously, in 1957, when the first classmen suspended the Ratline to protest the administration's order banning the intensification of Rat discipline that traditionally preceded the end of the Ratline and "Breakout." This period was known to every VMI man as "Resurrection." It was the last big push before the Rats charged up the stairwells, through the rest of the Corps and, when they reached the fourth stoop, were no longer a Rat mass, but the newest class of VMI cadets. Resurrection was as tough, in its own way, as Cadre Week and it was, in the eyes of the first class, a crucial element of the whole VMI ritual.

The suspension of Rat discipline in the barracks for two weeks that spring of 1957 led to a reexamination of the VMI way of doing things by a special commission appointed by the Board of Visitors. The Ratline survived, of course, with some modifications—it is always being modified, and some VMI men are always unhappy with the results. It had happened before, even during the period when General John Lejeune was Superintendent and made the elimination of hazing—which in those days included actual beatings—a priority of his administration. Lejeune had commanded the second division of the American Expeditionary Force during World War I and then served as Commandant of the Marine Corps, and nobody could accuse him of being soft on discipline. At VMI, the distinction between hazing (arbitrary punishment) and tough military discipline (the Ratline) is endlessly studied and argued over. And it is constantly evolving.

To outsiders and VMI's antagonists, this tension is a sign of weakness. VMI men recognize it as a sign of vitality: a measure of just how much they care. It is a family quarrel over what is best for the family. Outsiders couldn't possibly understand.

But the tension has to find outlets. Snowstorms provide one of the best opportunities to let off some of the accumulated steam. There is nothing like a good snowball fight for working out some of your frustrations. After a snowstorm, the missiles sail across the courtyard from every stoop and when you are walking to class, and least suspecting it, you can be ambushed and get your hat knocked off by a well aimed missile. It is routine to see someone walking around with a black eye that he got when he caught a snowball in the face. Those are the fortunes of war.

The mental and emotional pressures of VMI are undeniable and unrelenting for all cadets, and a lot of them learn that some hard physical exertion is a reliable way to relieve stress. You feel better when your body has the clean burning sensation that follows a hard workout. The running and the lifting isn't part of some competition: it's a way of holding your own.

There are the usual winter sports for those who play them. Varsity and club. Basketball. Wrestling. Out on the parade ground, when it is not covered with snow, there are men playing rugby in the mud. Down in the weight room, cadets work out on their own, pumping iron. And, always, out around the Post, there are cadets in sweats, running.

Rats, of course, do not have to worry about finding a physical release. There are plenty of first classmen—especially those on the RDC—who are only too happy to assign them pushups, mountain climbers, crunches and the like, to keep their bodies active and spirits clean.

The Rat Challenge course, in the hills and woods behind the Post, provides another way for cadets of all classes to work off some of the frustrations that seem to accumulate as winter lingers on. It feels good, on those days when the weather permits, to run up the hill, clapping and counting cadence, and then go through the obstacles. Rappelling gives you an adrenaline shot that lasts, at least, through SRC. And a couple of rounds with the pugil stick—whether you hit or get hit—leaves you with a good, clean feeling; ready for the books.

But for some cadets the only way to break the tension seems to be in breaking the rules. In fact the tradition of pranksterism and hell raising goes all the way back to the earliest days of the Institute to a colorful character named Ben Ficklin of the class of 1849. Among Ficklin's other accomplishments was that of being one of the founders of the Pony Express. While at VMI, he buried the Superintendent's boots in the snow, painted the same man's horse with zebra stripes, and detonated fireworks in the barracks. After being kicked out for lack of discipline, he enlisted in the Army and fought conspicuously in Mexico, where he was badly wounded. He then talked himself back into VMI, and when he graduated, he stuck his diploma on a bayonet.

His spirit lives on a century and a half later, nourished by one of the codes within codes. One cadet—whose son is a member of the class of '98—raised so much hell, including setting off fireworks and jumping from the fourth stoop into the laundry truck that was parked in the courtyard, that he was finally kicked out on demerits. He enlisted in the Army, went to OCS and Special Forces training, and returned to VMI to complete his degree. He wore his Green Beret while he was still, technically, a cadet. He is a distinguished graduate and will, almost certainly, make general officer rank.

Life at VMI is serious but it is bad form and bad strategy to take things too seriously. A sense of humor—whether it takes the form of pranks or simply an ability to laugh at the absurdities of the Ratline—is just about indispensable. So cadets do things to make themselves laugh. They march out of step when doing PTs. They come up with elaborate practical jokes—such as removing the wood panel from a BR's rack so that he falls through the floor when he lies down on his hay—and off-the-wall team sports like garbage-can-rolling in the sinks or broom hockey in a flooded and frozen courtyard of New Barracks. They bomb rooms with shaving cream. Launch missiles—chiefly water balloons—at the sentinel. Steal bathrobes from the showers. They invent nicknames and new ways to torment rats or provoke flamers to prove that a man hasn't lost his spirit.

At VMI there is no privacy. A cadet cannot withdraw into himself. The cadets make a virtue out of necessity: when you have no secrets you don't bother trying to keep any. There is a kind of easy intimacy about life in the barracks. The bull sessions are endless and seamless. Cadets enter each other's rooms and simply sit down and talk. You talk about everything; share everything (with the single exception of Honor Court proceedings, which are held in strict secrecy.) You begin to feel you know the men you live with better than anyone you'll ever know again. This bond makes it easy to laugh off the hardships that outsiders see in VMI.

"You just can't understand it unless you've been through it," cadets inevitably say. "but once you've been through it, you wouldn't trade it for anything."

One cadet, pondering graduation and life after VMI, said in a voice that was almost

forlorn: "I know when I leave this place, I'll never be this close to anyone again. After this, you're out there on your own."

In these short days and cold nights after Christmas—known as the Dark Ages around the Post—the Rats are still in the Ratline and still straining. Each day brings Breakout that much closer, and however long it is until that day, the Rats who have survived until now know that they can make it.

The third class, especially, is feeling its own kind of pressure. There has been a lot of academic attrition, and life on the third stoop seems only marginally better than the poor existence of last year, one floor up. Thirds—Rats with radios—have almost as much reason as the Rats to anticipate Breakout and the arrival of spring. They have few other distractions, and certainly not many privileges. After a few months, the right to wear a bathrobe when you are on the stoop does not seem like such a big deal.

And there is the business of getting through school. The academic pace is merciless, especially for the cadets who came to study what VMI has been traditionally noted for teaching: engineering. These technical subjects are hard disciplines, and require, if not more work, then certainly more sustained concentration than the liberal arts. (Which, it should be pointed out, VMI does not ignore. Josiah Bunting went from English major at VMI to Rhodes scholar at Oxford, one of nine VMI Rhodes scholars.)

There is never enough time, with labs and classes and the military demands of the I, to get it all done. At least not before lights out in barracks, at 2300. After lights out, cadets are allowed to stay until midnight in the library, or in some of the academic buildings, which are always open, until 0200, when every man is required to be in barracks. In the wee hours of cold January nights, you see cadets with bookbags hustling across the parade ground for Jackson Arch, hurrying to beat the deadline.

When they are back in barracks, some of them will crawl under blankets and continue studying, using a small flashlight to illuminate their books and notes. Still, some cadets fall behind and find themselves on academic probation, which means they lose whatever meager opportunities they had to get away from the Post and its strains. Conduct probation and academic probation are similar in that they both result in confinement—just what a man at VMI needs least when he's struggling. For some cadets, that feeling of being trapped makes the temptation to quit irresistible.

"You feel like you wouldn't mind working this hard," says a third classman who is struggling, "if you were having some fun. But this time of year, at this place, you've forgotten how to spell 'fun,' much less how to have any."

There is help, of course, for the man who is having academic difficulty. It is a small school and there is no lack of dedication among the faculty. But, as one of them once put it, "These young men are stoics. If they aren't born stoics, they become that way after they have been here for a while. You are expected to be tough, and asking for help is considered a sign of weakness. They'll do it, of course. But they don't like to and they'll wait until it is almost too late. Part of the ethos of this place is that it is hard, and sometimes these young men act as though they think they have to make it even harder than it is; that they have to be hard on themselves."

Many third classmen, during this season, wonder what it was they looked forward to about this year and wish there were some sort of academic equivalent of Breakout—a release.

For the seconds, this is a time of year when the class begins to organize itself for next year, when it will run the barracks. The selection process for positions of regimental rank has already begun. For the men who have military careers in mind, there is the summer to think about. Norfolk, Fort Bragg, Quantico, and Tyndall Air Force Base are some of the places where these men will be spending the summer, and they are already wondering about their orders. For these cadets the late winter days are full of significance. Regimental rank is important, even crucial. It is one thing to be a first class private if you are going to work for the bank. But if you plan on being a lieutenant and platoon leader in the Marine Corps, then you want those stripes. And any second classman who plans on graduate school needs the grades and the courses. This is suck-it-up time: time to start looking hard at the world beyond the I.

Of all the men in barracks, the first class has in some ways the heaviest burden. There is Breakout, which is up to them to organize and which will be a big part of their legacy. These are "their Rats," and they want them broken out right. No shortcuts; nothing that lets anyone say later that this Rat mass somehow got out easy. Official or not, "Resurrection"—that extra pressure on the Rats just before Breakout—still exists at VMI. But the first class also has eyes on the main prize—graduation, and life after VMI. Push too hard now, go too far during Resurrection, and you could find yourself in front of the Commandant or the Supe or, even, on the bus.

"Man, I've got too much riding," you will hear men say around Barracks, "to risk it all. They can break out without any help from me. I'm lying in the weeds."

A cadet who has just come back from a job interview in Roanoke and is thinking about his future with some engineering firm can have a hard time focusing on the Ratline or anything else.

Many of the firsts are distracted, and some of the Rats are shrewd enough to recognize it. There is a lot more tooling—Rats can be glimpsed slouching up and down the stairs as though they had no fear of anything—and this only drives the flamers to ratchet up their personal pressure.

Besides, there's a premature sense on the first stoop that it is all over. Men, especially those who will not be taking commissions, have already been released, in their minds, from the confinements of VMI. They may be here physically, but the rest of them is somewhere else. The weekends, the dates and parties, the plans for summer and beyond seem more important. A man who doesn't watch it can screw up, miss a bed check or get a "number one" for alcohol and find himself on confinement and marching PTs right up until the day, almost the very moment, he graduates. It happens every year. The last few weeks of first class year can be a dangerous time. Too many distractions. Too many temptations. Too much to think about.

Everybody—the whole Corps—needs some relief.

It comes in the form of Breakout.

Breakout

The first class decides (in discussions with the administration) on the exact day of Breakout. It cannot be too early for at least two reasons. First, because the Rats must not get off light; one of the torments of the Ratline is that it goes on until everyone is fed up. Second, because the weather has to be right. Warm enough, that is, so that Rats don't suffer from hypothermia. Breakout is bad enough without frostbite casualties.

So it won't be in January, and if it turns out to be in February, it won't be early February. Late in the month or, maybe, early March. The administration—weary of the Ratline and eager to get on with the straightforward educational mission of VMI— would prefer that it be early. The first classmen, determined that the Rats get the full benefit of the experience ("You aren't doing anyone any favors if somebody can say later that he got off easy as a Rat") want it to be later.

A compromise is worked out and though the date is supposedly secret, everyone— even the Rats—seems to know a week or two ahead of time.

As the day draws closer, the Rats who have managed to avoid being called in front of the RDC are issued invitations to attend what is called a "Virgin Night." No Rat will be allowed to make it through the year without putting in at least one appearance before the RDC.

"I pretty much knew what to expect," says a man who was invited to virgin night and is still sweating after the same ordeal his BRs have been going through. "By now, nobody is going to pee in his pants or faint away just because somebody yells at him and makes him strain and do some mountain climbers."

The Rats are salty. And ready.

So Resurrection begins, with early morning sweat parties. The first classmen give drop privileges to the seconds and thirds and leave the Post (except the few who are on confinement) for the weekend. The RDC, however, remains behind to conduct a forced march on Saturday afternoon. The march is attended by the Superintendent, the Commandant, the Academic Dean. It is a four hour march, with rifles carried at the port, and the pace is quick.

At the end of this march, the president of the RDC speaks to the Rats.

"You have come a long way," he says. "And the end is very near. Stay unified. Stay strong."

The Rats whoop it up on the bricks and head back into the barracks where the thirds and seconds are waiting.

There are more sweat parties, official and unofficial, over the next two days. Rats

Opposite:

Get 'em up, Rats. Get 'em up." First class president's workout.

are worked out in the courtyard after lunch and the scene is nothing short of pandemonium. All the routine exercises, with a few new twists: Rats running with other Rats slung over their shoulders in a fireman's carry, for instance. There is all the usual yelling and screaming; the familiar agonized grimaces of the men who are being worked out to the point of exhaustion and beyond.

But there is a kind of ritualistic atmosphere about the whole thing. The Rats are not having any fun, certainly, but they are not terrified either—not by a long shot. Some of those who aren't sobbing for breath are actually grinning. And so are some of the men doing the yelling, as though to say, "Ain't this is kick?"

This is nearly the end.

There is another forced march, 0300 Wednesday, on the bricks, rifles carried at the port. Again, the Supe, wearing a sporty jogging suit, is out in front with the first class President. The members of the RDC are along to provide inspiration. This march heads out through the Limits Gate, skirting the edge of W & L, where the Minks are sleeping safely in their beds, and then proceeds up through the deserted streets of Lexington. The Rats call cadence as they march, hoping to rattle the windows at W & L and in town, waking up everyone who isn't fortunate enough to be out marching with this little band of Rat Brothers on this frosty, clear Virginia morning.

Three hours later, the Rats, still in good formation, march back across the W & L campus. They have lost only a handful of men to blisters, cramps, and exhaustion. Some of these are riding in the bed of a pickup truck begging the RDC members to let them get out and finish the march on foot.

Nothing doing.

The men who are still marching, still following the Supe, are singing cadence and stepping out. As the companies come up to the Lee Chapel, where the great general's body lies in its crypt, they come to present arms. It was once a tradition that VMI men rendered a salute when they passed the chapel. The requirement was dropped after the school was integrated in 1968. But some cadets still choose to render the salute and this night, all of the Rats do.

The Rat mass returns through the Limits Gate as the first faint streaks of orange appear in the sky, and marches to the front of Barracks, past the statues of Jackson and Marshall, and comes to a halt in front of the Supe's quarters.

There, General Bunting, who was one of them himself not quite forty years ago and today marched the entire way with them, says a few words.

"Men," he says, with an unmistakable tone of affection, "you have come a long way. Not just tonight but over this whole year. And now, you are almost there. One more day and you will no longer be a Rat mass but the newest class of VMI men. These are days that you will never forget. You will never be closer to anyone, except your families, than you are to the people standing next to you tonight. Your Brother Rats. You should be proud. I am proud of you. Proud to be associated with you. Well done, men. Carry on."

After a cheer, the Rats march back to the barracks to endure another day—the last—of sweat parties and random, escalating harassment.

That day passes. And then a long night. And a morning when it is even harder than usual to stay awake through class. And then, after lunch, the Rats are moved into JM

Hall where the president of the first class will address them, just as he did a thousand years ago, on the night when the Old Corps returned.

There were 391 of you, then, First Class President Addison Hagan tells them.

And there are 327 now.

"You have one more hill to climb," he tells them. "I want to see you around the sentinel box after you've done it. I am motivated, Rats. Are you motivated?"

JM Hall fills with yells and the sounds of stamping feet. So loud you think it will shatter the leaded glass windows.

"We have decided that you are ready for Breakout."

Which everyone knew but still, when the words are spoken, the noise grows even louder.

Back into barracks. Not—as in the 60s and 70s—into a bone-breaking, hand-to-hand struggle up the stairwells through a mass of resisting upperclassmen. These days, it's into BDUs with rope belts and duct tape around the wrists and ankles. Then fall back out onto the bricks with clean gym dyke in a laundry bag. Ground the laundry bags and move, double time, to the rifle range area near the rappelling cliffs, where it will all happen.

It doesn't sound like anything very special when you describe it to a civilian. It is just a steep little hill made of exposed red clay. What you have to do is . . . get to the top of the hill.

But that hill is a very hard climb. Everything that can be done to make a little red clay hill hard to climb has been done, and there are several hundred young men who are there to make sure that it is even harder to climb than that.

A pumper truck from the local fire department has wet down the hill, and there is standing water on the flat ground in front of the hill. First classmen stand in the flat. Seconds and thirds at the top of the hill. Just beyond the crest of the hill is a shallow trench, full of water. Beyond that, trees and a place where the men who have finished the climb can towel off.

The First Battalion arrives. The firsts quickly push the Rats onto their faces and bellies, into the mud. The Rats know what to do—start crawling for the hill. They have to get to the hill, then climb up it.

Just low crawling through the mud to get to the hill takes some doing. There are firsts who will grab you by the ankles and pull you back. Who will gleefully push your face down into the thick, red mud.

"Keep your eyes closed. Keep moving. Get up that hill."

The air around you is full of screams, most of them incomprehensible. You have been told, over and over, to keep your eyes closed. You couldn't see anything if you opened them. You are covered thoroughly with thick, gritty mud.

You move, guided by the noise. It takes, maybe, ten minutes—though it feels vastly longer—to clear the flat ground and reach the bottom of the hill, where it gets really hard.

The seconds and thirds are above you. They are there to help you . . . and to hinder you. They don't want it to be too easy—which isn't likely—but they want everyone to make it. In this regard, Breakout is an elegantly brutal metaphor for the Ratline and, indeed, the entire VMI experience: it must be made very hard, but not too hard. Your BRs are all around you, groping and straining, and trying to find some way to get some purchase on the side of that goddamned hill which is nothing but slippery, greasy mud. You grab and pull and make a couple of feet, then slide back a yard.

Somebody above gives you a push. So does somebody below. The guy above wins.

Absolutely no question about it. You are losing ground. You try again. Feet on the shoulder of your BRs. Could be the shoulders, anyway. Could be something else. Nobody can see and nobody cares. You care only about getting up that hill. Breaking out of that tangle of bodies and that quagmire of mud and getting to the top of the miserable little hill.

The scene, for those who are watching, is mayhem. The mud is so thick that it is impossible to make out faces. These men are merely shapes. Clawing, writhing, bawling shapes.

Slowly some of them get close to the top and a few of their howling tormentors now begin to help them. They form chains of bodies with the last man holding out a hand and screaming, "Here. Reach. Come on, we haven't got all day. Stretch. Get up here. Keep moving."

One by one, the muddy figures make it to the top of the hill. They are thrown into the trench by men who say, "What class are you?"

"Class of 2000, Sir."

"Congratulations. You don't have to call me Sir anymore."

And the exhausted, bewildered man crawls out of the trench, onto dry ground where, by now, his Dyke has made it from down below and is waiting for a muddy embrace.

The hill has been climbed.

There are showers in Cocke Hall for the men—no longer Rats—who climbed the hill. But it will be a dozen or more showers before they stop finding bits of grit and clay hiding on—or in—their bodies. They change into clean gym dyke. Move down to the mess hall. And, then, at 1900 assemble on the bricks to march, accompanied by drums, in through Jackson Arch to the courtyard, assemble around the sentinel box and listen to one last talk—of congratulations, this time—from the first class president. Then they give their yells. For the first class—their Dykes—and for the seconds and thirds. And then, at last, for themselves.

There are some men who can't hold back, at this moment, and are actually crying. There have been tears before, since matriculation, but this is different. There has never been anything like this before.

They have made it.

Following pages:

To break out, you must climb this hill . . .

It will be nothing but thick, sticky mud.

But there will be people here to encourage you . . .

. . . **A**nd to help you make it to the top . . .

. . . **B**ecause you can't make it to the top alone. . . .

. . . **A**nd you won't be permitted to make it easily.

When you get to the top, there will be one final bath in the pit.

Congratulations!

The men who have just broken out (and cleaned up) enter Jackson Arch behind the drums . . .

. . . **A**nd assemble around the sentinel box for a talk by the first class president.

They give the old yells and then sing the "Doxology." Now they are the newest class at VMI.

Breakout

❖

New Market

In the spring, life at VMI becomes less grueling, though it never becomes entirely easy. The weather, of course, has something to do with this. The Valley turns green again, and after Spring Furlough, which closely follows Breakout, the uniform changes from gray wool to white cotton.

At taps, on the night the Corps returns to the Post, the first classmen bring their gray wool trousers, their woollies, to the sentinel box where they pile them up and set them on fire.

"It's almost impossible to believe," says one man who had just watched the trousers he'd worn for four years go up in flames, "that you'll never wear that uniform again."

So the first classmen are oddly subdued and contemplative as the flames climb. There is none of the exuberance of the old Rat days. They may shake hands and throw an arm around a BR's shoulder. But their mood is one of calm reflection. "You feel, for maybe the first time," one cadet says, "that it really is over—or will be, soon—and you kind of think, you know, about what it all means."

The rest of the Corps, however, yells and cheers as the flames climb twenty feet into the air. The newly designated fourth classmen are especially loud. It has something to do with being a part of this ritual, one of many that is peculiar to VMI. To an outsider, it might seem a little odd to burn your clothes in the first place, let alone make a ritual of the burning, with cheering and all.

But the woollies are not just clothes. They are part of the discipline of VMI. A cadet does not have the luxury of choosing what to wear when he gets up in the morning. Those gray wool trousers are just one more form of the cadet's confinement—a confinement that first classmen have been under four long years—and burning them is a form of release. Which might also explain why, when a cadet wears out a pair of smooth-toed, black shoes, he ties the laces together and slings them up into the branches of a tree, making it a "shoe tree." At VMI, you have an adversarial relationship with what you wear, and it feels like a small victory to be rid of it at last. The fire is hot and it smells. Some men swear they can smell it for days after and that the scent lingers around barracks until graduation.

In April the dogwoods bloom, and in the afternoon men drift out to the parade ground to throw baseballs and frisbees or to hit golf balls in the extra daylight and unaccustomed free time that comes with spring. Some take their books down to the stadium and sit in the bleachers—known as L.A. (Liberal Arts) Beach—studying

Opposite:

Signed photograph of General Robert E. Lee. Donated to VMI Museum by his daughter, Mildred.

while they soak up some sun. There appear to be more civilians around the Post now, many of them visiting coeds from the various schools around the state. There is something almost festive about the Friday afternoon parades.

A typical VMI cadet may not be much given to reflection over his entire four years at the I, but on the verge of graduation he usually begins to muse on the larger meaning of the place and his experience here. VMI does not necessarily breed poets—though the Superintendent is certainly a literary man and even old Stonewall Jackson himself had a touch of the poet about him. His last words before he died of wounds suffered at Chancellorsville, his greatest victory, are immortal: "Let us cross over the river and rest in the shade of the trees."

But reflection comes almost unbidden to the man who realizes that he is walking these grounds for the last time as a cadet. So much of what he has become happened here. And so much that happened before he ever came here has been preserved and handed down to make him the man that he has become. This place will always be a part of him; and part of him will always be here.

The landmarks seem to resonate even more than usual at this time of year. The statue of Jackson, the four cannons Jackson used when he trained cadets—Matthew, Mark, Luke, and John—the names on the walls. You cannot have passed through four years at VMI without absorbing some of this history, even if your conscious mind was always occupied by the pressures of the Ratline, classes, military duties, athletics, and the limited but all-important social life.

George Marshall spent four years here, and his statue stands in front of New Barracks, on the right flank of Jackson's. A cadet will have walked past it a thousand times without thinking once about the man and his remarkable, inspiring career. A cadet

Opposite page:

At New Market, John Ried was hit in the jaw by a Minnie ball. He had it made into a watch fob. Close-up against a Confederate battle flag. From the VMI museum.

Above:

The New Market battle streamer.

about to graduate and take a commission in the same army that Marshall once commanded, an army he turned from a small corps into the most powerful service in the world, will wonder about his own destiny. By Marshall's own account, VMI prepared him for the great things he accomplished. A man cannot consider Marshall without wondering if there are not great things in store for him too.

This sense of possibility mingles with any cadet's ruminations about the past. He recognizes names on the Cincinnatus Monument because some of the cadets he has known have those same names. Generation after generation from the same families have been here, been shaped here, and then gone out into the world. Four John Mercer Pattons graduated from the Institute. Two George S. Pattons. A third George S. Patton attended for one year before transferring to West Point and going on to glory as commander of the U.S. Third Army in World War II. That Patton once said, "Give me a group of men from The Citadel and I'll win a battle. Give me a bunch of men from VMI and I'll win a war."

The crux of all VMI history, of course, is New Market—the battle, the legend, the town, the ritual. A cadet is reminded of New Market every day he is on Post when he walks by the somber figure of *Virginia Mourning Her Dead* and the graves, beneath the statue, of six of the ten VMI cadets killed in that battle.

Many VMI men have died in combat, from the Civil War to Desert Storm, where two VMI men were KIA. VMI trains citizen soldiers and soldiers are expected to fight, and sometimes, to die. It is their duty, and VMI teaches duty if nothing else. If you told a graduating cadet that some of his BRs would be dead in a few years, casualties of war, he would not be surprised. VMI men are everywhere the United States military goes.

Even against this sober background, the story of New Market is something different. The New Market cadets were not citizen soldiers so much as schoolboy soldiers. It was 1864, and the South was holding on, everywhere on the defensive. The war had become far more destructive, much more cruel than anyone could have imagined. But as they marched the eighty miles from Lexington to New Market, the cadets slipped out of camp at night to dance with the ladies in towns along the route. To these young men, war was still an adventure, and it could have been 1861, before Manassas.

Every cadet knows the story. The Rats visited New Market battlefield at the very start of the year, on that Sunday that marked the end of Cadre Week and the return of the Old Corps. On Sunday morning they rode down the valley in buses, wearing whites without shoulder board insignia. The Cadre who rode the buses with them had been told to go easy. This trip was for reflection, not harassment.

Three days earlier, the first class president and some of his staff had left the Post for New Market, on foot, carrying a guidon and an Alice pack loaded with the shoulder insignia that the Rats would put on later—after they had walked the battlefield and charged up the same small hill that the New Market cadets assaulted during the Battle of New Market. The cadets who made the historic charge in that spring of 1864 had been called out of barracks by General John Breckenridge. They were to be his reserve in the fight against the numerically superior army of Franz Sigel which, if not stopped, would have threatened Robert E. Lee's left flank and might have cost the Confederacy the war.

From Lexington to New Market is a long march, then and now. In fall of 1996 many of the VMI first classmen had just returned from a summer at Quantico or Fort

Bragg, and were able to march the course in the same three days that it had taken the New Market cadets that May of long-ago, when they had moved among gaunt Confederate veterans who would cradle their muskets and taunt them with strains of "Rock a Bye Baby."

The insignia in the first classmen's Alice pack were in some sense sanctified by the re-enactment of the march. When the Rats pinned on those insignia, they were being asked to continue a sacred trust.

Though few at the moment could say how or why, somehow the deep pride that the New Market tradition evokes in every VMI man had already been stirred for the first time: the Rats marched through the town of New Market behind a Rat band, more competently than the training they had received during Cadre Week could have accounted for.

On the Post, eight months later, the entire Corps pays its annual homage to the New Market tradition. It is always on the anniversary of the battle—May 15—and it is the most important, most deeply ceremonial event in the VMI calendar.

By May a parade is a routine event, and the cadets bring a kind of cocky attitude to the rehearsals. They march well enough, but they are plainly doing it by the numbers, and they take a kind of pleasure in fouling up in small ways that bring down the wrath

Above:

Dinner party at the Supe's in honor of graduation.

of the observing TACs and members of the administration. One of the best games is to mispronounce the names of the cadets who fell at New Market during the report.

"Private Cabell," a cadet sings out, putting the emphasis on the wrong syllable at a rehearsal a day or two before the actual parade.

"No, no, no," shouts an officer from the administration.

The Corps snickers.

Everyone knows how to pronounce the name properly. Every Rat has to learn those ten names. Every cadet knows them by heart; knows the story of how the cadets, some 250 of them, were the reserve in Breckinridge's line when a gap opened and Sigel was plainly on the verge of exploiting it. An officer rode to Breckinridge with the news and pleaded, "General, why don't you put the cadets in line." The VMI boys were still in reserve, where Breckinridge wanted them.

Would they stand, he asked.

The officer assured him that they would.

Breckinridge had dreaded this moment from the moment he requested the assistance of the VMI cadets, and brooded over it for the rest of his life. Some of his staff officers said later that they saw tears in his eyes as he considered the decision.

"Put the boys in," he said, finally, "and may God forgive me for the order."

The cadets moved forward, behind their flag. They had been under fire earlier, but it was nothing like this. A shell landed in the middle of one company, killing two of the cadets instantly and mortally wounding a third. The cadets closed up and continued their advance. Another cadet was killed by a musket ball a little further on.

Colonel Ship, in command at the head of the formation, was hit. The wound initially looked serious, perhaps mortal. The advance stalled briefly, but another officer rallied the cadets and they moved forward through an orchard and then, at last, to the relative security of a rail fence.

They had filled the gap in Breckinridge's line. Schoolboys.

A storm, which had covered the battlefield all day, reached a new level of fury. Lightning and thunder now added their impact to the driving rain. Sigel's attack had been broken and now, in the midst of this storm, the entire line of Confederate troops—including the VMI cadets—rose and attacked.

The cadets advanced through a section of low ground full of standing water and deep, clinging mud that sucked the shoes off some of their feet. In the lore, this forlorn little depression became the "field of lost shoes." Their objective was a battery of Union guns. The cadets bore down on it remorselessly. An officer in command of one of the units on their flank said, in admiration, that their charge "surpassed anything that I witnessed during the war."

A wounded Federal officer later wrote of their advance, "No one who saw it will ever forget it. No command but one most admirably drilled and disciplined could have done it."

The Union artillerymen abandoned a twelve pounder on the field, which the cheering, exhilarated cadets promptly captured. It was the high water moment of their war and, perhaps, their lives; the stuff of legend. The schoolboys had triumphed.

Breckinridge ordered the cadets out of the line but not before one of them had taken twenty-three Union soldiers prisoner. The cadets had suffered almost 25 percent casualties. An emotional Breckinridge rode to their position and spoke to them.

"Young gentlemen," he said, "I have you to thank for the result of today's operations." Then, he added, "Well done, Virginians . . . well done, men."

In Preston Library, there are several copies of an early history of the battle, one of which is inscribed:

WILLIAM P UPSHUR
VIRGINIA MILITARY INSTITUTE, CLASS 1902

From his father:
John Nottingham Upshur
Co C New Market Battalion
Virginia Military Institute, Class 1864

Upshur senior was wounded so severely in the leg during the battle that he was unable to return to VMI. He later became a prominent physician. His son, who became a Marine officer after graduating from VMI, went on to win the Medal of Honor.

The lives of all the New Market cadets are recorded in another volume, found in the VMI library. Reading the entries one realizes that these young men were, in Oliver Wendell Holmes' phrase, truly "touched by fire."

One of the New Market cadets, Thomas Gordon Hayes, became mayor of Baltimore.

Charles James Faulkner, who took the twenty-three prisoners, became, among other things, a U.S. senator.

William Fountain Battie became an Arkansas sheriff and was killed while trying to make an arrest.

William H. Kennedy Jr., like several other New Market cadets, served with Mosby after New Market.

John Bransford fought in the battle of Santiago as a U.S. Navy surgeon.

Thomas Stapes Martin became minority leader in the U.S. Senate.

George Raum was an author and Egyptologist whose extraordinary career included such events as being saved from a firing squad by Mosby's Rangers; riding with Mosby; meeting Stanley, Rhodes, and Kitchener in Africa; participating in the discovery and excavation of the Great Sphinx; and other exploits that come from living the life of Indiana Jones.

Erskine Mayo Ross became a prominent rancher and lawyer, and a fabled judge in Los Angeles.

Charles William Turner became adjutant general of Montana and was later assassinated in Seattle.

Franklin Graham Gibson—who suffered seven wounds at New Market (he had one leg shattered and took a ball through the other thigh, took another ball through the hand costing him two fingers, and yet another in the cheek)—taught French and mathematics at Richmond College, and became a lawyer and prosecuting attorney.

Moses Ezekiel organized the Red Cross in Italy during the First World War. He was also a sculptor of international fame and was entitled to call himself "Sir Moses Ezekiel." However, his stone in Arlington National Cemetery reads merely:

Moses J. Ezekiel
Sergeant of Company C, Battalion of Cadets
of the
Virginia Military Institute

In 1906, Ezekiel's monument *Virginia Mourning Her Dead* was dedicated on the grounds of VMI.

The Corps marches in full dyke—coatees, crossed dykes, shakos—for the New Market parade. When the report is taken, those ten names are called out again, remembered again.

"Corporal Atwill."

"Corporal Atwill died on the field of honor, Sir."

"Private Haynes."

"Private Haynes died on the field of honor, Sir."

"Private Jefferson."

"Private Jefferson died on the field of honor, Sir."

And so on. Until all the names have been called.

The covenant that every country, every Army, makes with the men it sends into battle is that their sacrifice will never be forgotten. VMI keeps its promise. A wreath is laid at the base of Sir Moses Ezekiel's statue. A firing party renders a three-volley salute. The pipes play "Amazing Grace," and when the last, mournful note has died, taps is played, with an echo bugler answering from New Barracks across the parade ground.

The moment honors the dead. A hush falls over the Post. A few spectators wipe away tears. Then the Corps passes in review, marching for the only time down the street instead of the parade ground. This moment, in its way, celebrates both the living and the dead. The cadets who survived New Market and went on to live extraordinary lives. The cadets who died in other wars. Those who survived. Those "citizen soldiers" who never served in battle but whose lives were molded by VMI. The first classmen who receive their diplomas tomorrow, some of whom will be commissioned in the military, with senior officers who are VMI graduates here to swear them in. The second classmen who will run the Corps next year and the thirds who will return to get their rings. The fourth classmen who survived the Ratline.

The Corps passes in review for the last time this year. The Institute, imposing as always, remains the same. But it has changed every one of them forever.

Opposite:

Brian Bagwan, first captain and regimental commander, 1996–97, in front of the painting of New Market charge in JM Hall.

Following pages:

The New Market battlefield. The cadets formed behind this fence to charge the cannons on the high ground.

Marching to New Market the way the Corps did it in 1864. In these cadets' packs: the Rats' shoulder crests.

Rats, having toured the New Market battlefield and re-created the Corps' charge across the "Field of Lost Shoes," pin on their crests.

The Rats march through the town of New Market (behind cadets from the VMI Civil War round-table dressed as Confederate troops) in their first parade as cadets.

New Market Day parade on the Post.

Remembering the fallen.

The swearing in of new ensigns and VMI graduates.

The VMI Uniform

❖

Like most things at VMI, the uniform seldom changes. A cadet today routinely wears uniforms that make him look like one of those men who took over the old arsenal 160 years ago.

The uniform back then was the coatee. It resembled the uniform at West Point, itself copied from the blue dress uniform of the "Young Guard" of France (West Point had decided to use gray as a way of honoring General Winfield Scott, whose victorious troops at the Battle of Chippewa in 1814 had worn gray uniforms).

The coatee is still gray but it is no longer worn to class, as it was for the first sixty years of VMI's history when it was *the* uniform, worn for virtually all occasions on Post.

Colonel Francis Smith paid close attention to the quality and cost of the uniform, and in his annual report to the Board of Visitors in 1842, he wrote that he had "…found it necessary to take immediate steps to procure suitable clothing for the cadets. The cloth furnished by the merchants of Lexington was not only inferior in quality but it was absolutely worthless; every coat, it is believed, which is made for the third class having been threadbare in little more than a few weeks." Smith "went to the North," and found a supplier of uniforms whose wool was "nearly $1.00 per yard cheaper than that furnished by the Lexington merchants."

VMI uniforms are still made in "the North." In Philadelphia, as it happens, and before that, in New York. They are still wool—18 to 18½ ounce Kersey—which is a bit lighter than the wool in the original uniforms, though the price is a lot more than the $3.00 a yard Francis Smith was prepared to pay.

In 1890, the coatee was replaced as the normal duty uniform by the gray blouse which, according to the 1890 regulation, was to be "of gray cloth, conforming closely to the shape of the wearer, but not tight fitting, to button in front with a single row of five flat, black buttons underneath a fly." The coatee did not disappear, but became the uniform for formal and ceremonial occasions.

In 1957, the regulation blouse was changed to this extent: a zipper replaced buttons—probably because a number of cadets had unauthorized, but convenient, zippers sewed in to replace the buttons. A zipper could save a man a quarter of a minute getting ready for formation.

The gray blouse remained the standard duty uniform until after World War II, when the class uniform appeared. The gray blouse, like the coatee before it, became a uniform for more formal occasions. "The evolution of the uniform has, over the years, been a trend toward specialization," says Colonel Keith Gibson, Director of the VMI Museum. "Where you had one uniform, or two, for all occasions, now it seems you have a uniform for every occasion." At VMI there are many occasions—from Breakout to Sunday church—and as the preceding following pages show, there is a uniform for every one of them.

Uniform identifications

A. *Drum major dyke. Coatee, ducks. Joseph Klapatch.*
1. *O.D. dyke with cape. Winter. Steven Jones.*
2. *Idiot dyke. Worn by Rats during Cadre Week. Justin Pusczykowski.*
3. *Social dyke. Warm weather. Michael Russell.*
4. *White blouse. Warm weather. James Johnston.*
5. *Full dyke with arms, overcoat. Non-com. John Dewey.*
6. *Overcoat with woollies. Matthew Neely.*
7. *Coatee full dyke with arms. Darius Parker.*
8. *Full dyke with arms. Matthew Milburn.*
9. *Travel dyke. William Smith.*
10. *Coatee full dyke with arms. Officer. David Short.*

B. *Color sergeant. Coatee, white ducks, full dyke with arms. Warm weather. Dan Gibson.*
1. *Guard dyke, sentinel. Warm weather. John Denton.*
2. *Sweat dyke. Daniel Owens.*
3. *Rain cape and cap cover. Jeffrey Morrison.*
4. *Pep Band dyke. Joel Christenson.*
5. *Sentinel dyke with cold weather hat, with arms, cape back. Joseph Bartolomeo.*
6. *Sentinel dyke with cold weather hat, with arms, cape down. Joseph Bartolomeo.*
7. *Gym dyke. Jason Middough.*
8. *Class dyke with black sweater. Winter. Jason Mitchell.*
9. *Monogram sweater. Winter. Thomas Haskins —consensus 1AA All-American.*
10. *O.D. dyke. Winter. William J. Scott.*

C. *Color sergeant full dyke with Corps flag, with arms. Overcoat. Mark Pruitt.*
1. *Color corporal. Gordon Overby.*
2. *Full dyke with arms. Eric Mowles.*
3. *Bathrobe. Dave Sullivan.*
4. *Rat Challenge dyke. John Herrin.*
5. *Officer dyke with overcoat. Hompeng Komthirath.*
6. *Class dyke. Winter. Keith Lawhorn.*
7. *Class dyke. Warm weather. Pol Ou.*
8. *Company cadre dyke. Kristopher Turpin.*
9. *Full dyke with arms, saber-bearing NCO. Winter. Mark Glancy.*
10. *Guidon parade dyke. Summer. Shannon Ferguson.*

D. *Color sergeant full dyke with arms. Joseph Seiler.*
1. *RDC dyke. Spring. David Hudock.*
2. *Big Red Club dyke. Winter. Brian Skusa.*
3. *Block-running dyke. Kihwan Kim.*
4. *Monogram sweater. Warm weather. Carlton Mason.*
5. *Parade dyke NCO. Winter. Paul Staton.*
6. *Guard orderly dyke. Winter. Paul Staton.*
7. *Band dyke with meliophone. Joel Christenson.*
8. *Spirit squad dyke. Nakia Young.*
9. *Lab dyke. Paul Brown.*
10. *O.D. dyke. Dave Hudock.*

E. *1st Captain and Regimental Commander. Brian Bagwan.*
1. *Band dyke with drums. Summer. Matthew Baldwin.*
2. *Full dyke with arms. NCO. Summer. Geoffrey Alexander.*
3. *Class dyke with duty jacket. Winter. Keith Lawhorn.*
4. *Band dyke. Summer. Matthew Bertsch.*
5. *Gray blouse. Summer. Matt Vanhoose.*
6. *Gray blouse. Winter. With black gloves. Michael Wright.*
7. *Officer parade dyke. Early fall. Joseph Ryan Shy.*
8. *Church dyke. Winter. Chad Novacek.*
9. *Old Corps dyke. Gregory Russell.*
10. *Breakout dyke. Nathan Friedline.*

F. *Bagpipe dyke. Pipe major. George 'Donnie' Hasseltine.*
1. *Officer dyke with arms. Winter. Michael Russell.*
2. *EMT dyke. David Nash.*
3. *Band dyke with herald trumpet. Winter. Ryan Betton.*
4. *Band dyke. Coatee, white ducks. Summer. Travis Quesenberry.*
5. *Practice parade dyke. Winter. Clayton McVay.*
6. *Church dyke. Summer. Charles Marr.*
7. *Full parade dyke with arms. Summer. Joseph Carter.*
8. *Social dyke. Winter. Jason Trubenbach.*
9. *Rat Challenge cadre dyke. Sean Ting.*
10. *Saber-bearing NCO full dyke with arms. Summer. Brook Barbour.*

A

B

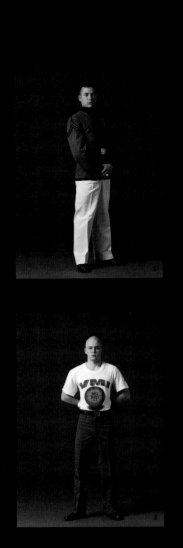

D

E

F

PORTRAITS

General J.H. Binford Peay III

❖

General J. H. Binford Peay III, United States Army, is the Commander-in-Chief of U.S. Central Command, responsible for military operations and the country's vital interests in southwest Asia. Selection to four stars in 1993 made him the highest ranking active duty graduate of VMI. Among the many awards and mementos on the wall of his office at MacDill Air Force Base in Tampa, Florida, is a framed sign that reads "MSR New Market."

The sign is a memento from the days when Peay commanded the 101st Airborne during Operation Desert Storm. "An officer under my command, who was a Citadel graduate, told me that his unit, which would be called 'Task Force Citadel,' would proceed up 'Main Supply Route New Market' to establish a large re-supply position for our division's movement against Iraqi forces. After the cease-fire, the troops gave me their road sign as a souvenir of the operation." Even in the deserts of Iraq and Saudi Arabia, the Institute has been a part of Peay's life.

His father was a 1929 graduate of VMI. He has a son, Jim, who is a member of the class of '98 and another, Ryan, who is "seriously thinking about attending." Peay gave the Ring Figure address to the class of '98 and addressed the class of '97 as they received their diplomas. Peay, himself, graduated in 1962. He studied civil engineering, was a cadet battalion commander, and received the Cincinnati Medal at graduation. But until two weeks before he graduated, he was unsure as to whether he would take a regular or reserve commission.

"The Commandant of Cadets, Jeffrey Smith—who was a Lieutenant Colonel then and became a general later—was tough and demanding, but also a fair and respected man. He stayed after me and finally persuaded me to take the regular commission. He was one of many strong influences on me at VMI, along with my father and General James Morgan, who was the revered Dean of the Civil Engineering department and Coach John McKenna, our outstanding football coach."

So Peay took his regular commission and five years later was in Vietnam for the first of two tours. He was with the Fourth Infantry Division in the Central Highlands in heavy combat at a series of firebases, including one called Brillo Pad, where the fighting was especially tough. While he does not talk too much about those days, he does say, "The experience of being at a firebase when it is being heavily shelled or overrun is something you don't forget. The lessons are clear."

In Vietnam the things he learned at VMI became even more important. They sustained him through combat. "It comes down, in the words of General Marshall, to 'how you live among men.' How you live in the barracks, among your classmates, on the athletic field and in the classroom. How you work with people; your reputation for being there when you have to be there. All that comes out of the crucible of VMI. When I was in Vietnam, what carried me many times was what I had learned at VMI. I didn't have to think about it; it was there."

Before Vietnam, he was still unsure about whether or not to make a career out of the army. But after Vietnam he made up his mind to stay. Again, he felt the old stirrings of lessons he had learned back at VMI—you don't quit simply because things have gotten difficult; the individual is less important than the unit and the objective; personal honor is always more important than personal gain.

"I thought the United States Army was in trouble," Peay says, simply, "and this was not the time to leave."

So he remained with the army through some of its most difficult years . . . a time of low morale, indiscipline, severe cutbacks, and a profound rethinking of purpose. There was another tour in Vietnam, during the last stages of the withdrawal; then a series of assignments that took him from personnel duties in Washington, to field command in Hawaii, to the Command and General Staff College at Fort Leavenworth, Kansas.

In 1990 he was made commanding general of the 101st Airborne at Fort Campbell, Kentucky. A year later he was vacationing at Virginia Beach with his family when he got the call telling him that Iraqi troops had invaded Kuwait.

"I spent the next nine months on the desert floor," he says.

During Desert Storm, his division moved ninety-five miles in one day, and sixty-five the next, to cut off the Republican Guard. It was the kind of dramatic, audacious maneuver that inevitably brings up comparisons with Stonewall Jackson's flanking march at Chancellorsville. On that day Jackson, noticing the number of officers in his command who were products of VMI, made this observation: "The Institute will be heard from today." It was. And it has been ever since.

What is it that the Institute gives to commanders like Peay?

"Well, it isn't that VMI people are smarter than anyone else," he says. "The Institute teaches you how to organize, manage time, break down a problem, and think under pressure and always with honor. Also, you take from VMI a base of wisdom that you learn from life in that barracks. That is where is all happens; where the important lessons are learned."

Superintendent Josiah Bunting III

This is the greatest job in the world, as far as I am concerned," says Josiah Bunting III, thirteenth Superintendent of Virginia Military Institute, as he covers the parade ground in long strides, making his way from the office to the barracks, "and I will stay here as long as they will have me. You don't always get a chance to give something back and this is my chance. I cannot calculate how much I owe to VMI."

General J. H. Binford Peay III,

United States Army, VMI class of

'62, stands at the window of his

office at MacDill Air Force Base in

Tampa, Florida. In 1997 General

Peay was the highest ranking, active

duty graduate of VMI.

Major General Josiah Bunting III,

the thirteenth Superintendent, VMI

class of '63, in the midst of Rats.

If Bunting feels fortunate, then so does the Institute. He is one of its most distinguished and versatile graduates. Soldier, educator, author, musician, athlete—a man of many parts and many accomplishments. He can quote Thucydides, effortlessly and without ostentation. But he also speaks the kind of language that cadets understand. "Yes," he says to one, who complains (respectfully) in an ad hoc gripe session about some minor irritant, "I remember we had to put up with the same kind of horseshit when I was here. I'll look into it."

Bunting arrived at VMI in 1959 from the Marine Corps, in which he had enlisted, and departed in 1963 for Oxford, as one of nine men in the Institute's history to win a Rhodes Scholarship. Along the way, he distinguished himself as cadet first captain and regimental commander, member of the Honor Court, and co-captain of the swimming team. After two years at Oxford—where he took an honors in modern history—he left academe for his other life, as a soldier. His army career was short but active and included tours as a company commander in the Eighty-Second Airborne and with the Ninth Infantry Division in the Mekong Delta of Vietnam, where he earned the Bronze Star with two oak leaf clusters.

As in many who served there, the Vietnam experience struck a deep chord in Bunting. Unlike most, he had the talent to translate the experience into a novel. *The Lionheads,* published in 1972, was called one of the year's ten best books by *Time* magazine. By the time it was published, Bunting had left the army, having risen to the rank of major and served on the faculty of the United States Military Academy at West Point, where he taught history.

After his army service, Bunting became president of Briarcliff College; then president of Hampton Sydney College; and, before his appointment to VMI, headmaster of the Lawrenceville School. His was a distinguished academic resume, enhanced by awards, publications, and degrees. *Time* (again) called him one of "two hundred leaders for the future," and when the Institute needed new leadership, in 1995, he was chosen unanimously by the Board of Visitors.

"Supe" Bunting takes an obvious delight in his job. He visits football practice regularly and stalks the sidelines during games, shouting encouragement and pounding backs. He is at the head of the column when the Rats make their forced marches. He eats in the mess hall. During the long, wearing days that followed the Supreme Court ruling on the admission of women, Bunting growled to one visitor, "The worst part is that I'm now spending more time in little rooms, with lawyers, than I am with the cadets, in Barracks."

It is plain that, in Bunting's mind, the best part of his job is where life at VMI is truly lived—in the barracks. And when he strolls the courtyard, talking with the cadets, it is also plain that he is no stranger there. They know who he is and, more to the point, he knows who they are. They are his responsibility and, he says, "I admire their toughness. It is much harder for them, in their time, than it was for me. Not in the sense that the Ratline is harder but in the sense that the outside world is so much less interested and respectful of what they do. It is so much easier for them to say, 'To hell with this, it's not worth it.' They are an inspiration to me."

And he, of course, to them.

Described once as "first and foremost a teacher," Bunting still teaches English Literature. When the discussion during one class period in 1997 turned to the Victorians and Matthew Arnold, he asked his students, "What is culture? Give me an example of a type of culture?"

When, after some discussion, one cadet suggested that one example of culture might be "life in the barracks," Bunting nodded and smiled.

"Exactly. A good example. Life in the barracks. And a very singular culture, at that. It isn't the culture of the mall or television or the Ralph Lauren ads for clothes called 'Polo,' is it? It is a culture that would be alien to most people, but that is utterly familiar to a few who feel very strongly about it, isn't it? To them, it is a culture that is eminently worth preserving, worth sacrificing and fighting for, right?"

His students — his men — know that there is only one right answer to that question.

Robert H. Patterson Jr.

When he became only the ninth man to receive VMI's highest honor, the New Market Medal, on May 15, 1994, Robert H. Patterson Jr. also received the usual words of praise from VMI's twelfth Superintendent, General John W. Knapp. Patterson was especially grateful for those kind words, since he well remembered an earlier time when "another superintendent, General Charles Kilbourne, had some bad things to say about me."

"I was dismissed from this place for continual disregard of regulations," explains Patterson, with typical modesty, grace, and good humor. What General Kilbourne (who served as VMI's sixth Superintendent, from 1939 to 1946) had said, Patterson continues, "was entirely warranted." That was in 1945. Patterson left the Institute to enlist in the Navy, and though he returned to Lexington a wiser and more mature man and ended up serving on the Honor Court and as class historian (class of '49), he could not in his wildest imagination have dreamed of the long and arduous service he would eventually give to VMI in what became known, simply, as "the court case."

It began in 1989 when, according to court papers, a woman from somewhere in northern Virginia discovered her application to VMI would not be considered. VMI was for men only. When she complained, the U.S. Justice Department filed suit.

By then, Patterson was already one of Virginia's most distinguished attorneys. He had graduated from University of Virginia Law School as president of his class and editor of the *Virginia Law Review*, served as president of the Virginia State Bar and chairman of McGuire, Woods, Battle & Boothe in Richmond, one of the Southeast's largest law firms. He had also served the Institute as president of both the VMI Alumni Association and the VMI Board of Visitors.

For the next six years he would serve the school, which had once dismissed him, as chief counsel in a costly legal battle against the full force of the federal government. The case cost VMI more than ten million dollars and brought the Institute a kind of unwelcome prominence in a great national debate about the role — and future — of single sex education, women in the military, the concept of federalism, and other deeply divisive issues. It was a hard fight and though he waged it like the happy warrior that he is, it took a toll. "Bob Patterson," says Superintendent Josiah Bunting, "gave everything he had because he believed in VMI and he believed he was right. He conducted

Robert H. Patterson Jr., class of '49,
one of Virginia's most distinguished
attorneys, led the long legal battle
that ended with the Supreme Court
decision of 1996, opening VMI to
women.

❖

himself like an honorable man, in accord with the highest standards of the Institute."

And he won the first round. In 1991, a U.S. District Court Judge ruled in favor of VMI, saying that while the school may "march to the beat of a different drummer," it served an important state function and did not violate the Constitution.

The Justice Department appealed that decision. Patterson went back to court and was again successful.

In October 1992, the Fourth Circuit Court kicked the case back to the district court and gave it four options. VMI could: a) let women in; b) turn itself into a private college; c) create an equivalent program for women; or d) find some other solution.

Almost a year later, when VMI and the state of Virginia created the Virginia Women's Institute for Leadership at Mary Baldwin College, Patterson again played a key role. The program was not designed to re-create the Ratline, but would instead stress "positive reinforcement." In May 1994, the District Court judge who originally ruled in favor of VMI accepted the plan.

The Justice Department did not, and appealed.

In January 1995, a three judge panel from the Fourth circuit ruled 2–1 in VMI's favor.

The fight, by now, had become a national story. Patterson described it as "a fight pure and simple to destroy what VMI stands for. What we stand for—love of country and family, patriotism, duty, honor, a willingness to endure adversity and to overcome it—are anathema to our adversaries."

The Justice Department appealed the lower court's ruling to the U.S. Supreme Court. In January 1996, the Court heard arguments. Patterson did not himself argue the case in front of the court. He may well regret that decision, but even his formidable debating skills would likely not have been enough. VMI lost in a 7–1 ruling. (Justice Clarence Thomas excused himself since his son was, at the time, a VMI cadet).

"It was," says Patterson through a cloud of pipe smoke, "not unexpected. But still, it was a sad day. One of the saddest of my life."

He is sitting in his corner office, overlooking Richmond. The office is cluttered with mementos and keepsakes, many of them from VMI. Though VMI ultimately—and, perhaps, inevitably—lost the case, Patterson is not a pessimist or a defeatist. "This place," he says, pointing to a photograph of the barracks with the stem of his pipe, "has meant everything to me. I like to think that we fought the good fight. And I believe the principles we fought for will endure."

Thomas A. Saunders, III

When Thomas A. Saunders, III arrived on Wall Street in 1967, the firm that hired him, Morgan Stanley, was a small private partnership, consisting of perhaps fifteen partners and two hundred employees. Indeed, the entire world of investment banking was somewhat parochial and archaic, doing things the way it had for decades. Over the next twenty years, however, that world went through a sea change and Morgan Stanley became one of the leading institutions in the global financial industry.

"In 1970, when I was first in the syndicate department," Saunders says, "I kept the firm's capital position on a yellow pad. It was about eight million dollars. Today it is about twelve billion!"

If he is an insider now, in the early days he was a kind of double anomaly on Wall Street. First, there were not many southerners on the Street. "The old, eastern money Ivy League network ran the place back then," Saunders remembers, still speaking with the soft, lilting Tidewater drawl—he comes from Ivor, a small town near Norfolk—"and people would look at you now and then in a way that meant they thought you talked funny."

And while southerners were rare enough on Wall Street, VMI men were even more scarce. "There probably weren't more than three of us in the whole investment banking business," Saunders says.

That is not to say that VMI had not prepared Saunders for Wall Street. "It was an invaluable experience," he says. "One that prepared me to succeed in life . . . though I wasn't a great success while I was at the Institute. I had good grades, but I was actually something of a rebel, always testing the system . . . which is, at best, a nice way of putting it. One night, some of us studying electrical engineering wired our stereo into the barracks PA system, and no one knew where the blaring rock and roll was coming from.

"So I walked a ton of PTs. As many PTs as I marched, I probably could have walked from Lexington to Norfolk and back in my Rat year alone. All the shenanigans resulted in my ending up a first class private, but I believe it also was an important part of what I took away from VMI."

He graduated in electrical engineering in 1958. "I had to work hard," he remembers, "and that was an invaluable lesson: discipline and hard work are critical components of success. Couple these with integrity and a little luck, and you have the formula for success no matter what you choose to do."

From VMI, Saunders went into the army where, he recalls with a smile, "Infantry school at Fort Benning was a snap after VMI."

From Benning, he went to Fort Knox, and after leaving the army, he worked in private industry, before earning his MBA at the University of Virginia's Darden School and moving on—to Morgan Stanley and the world of global finance and mega-deals.

In his distinguished twenty-two year career at Morgan Stanley, Saunders became one of the firm's senior Managing Directors. Over the years, he provided financial advice and managed many noteworthy transactions for the likes of AT&T, DuPont, General Motors, Exxon, and British Telecom. In the late 80s, as Chairman of Morgan Stanley's private equity fund, he was responsible for over two billion dollars of capital raised from a worldwide network of institutional partners.

In 1989, Saunders left Morgan Stanley to found his own private equity firm—Saunders Karp & Megrue—which invests its own and its partners' capital in a diversified portfolio of companies spanning a variety of industries. His partners include AT&T, Bell Atlantic, General Electric, the University of California, and Mitsubishi, among others. From his office on Madison Avenue, high enough to offer an expansive view of Central Park, he can reflect on the lessons he learned at VMI and how they helped him survive and prosper on the Street.

"Well, you learn that you cannot walk away from responsibility. If there is a problem, then you are going to have to deal with it. The question of success comes up all the time. People want to know how you become successful in this business because it is intensely competitive, with everyone scrambling to get to the top. Unfortunately, people often measure it in terms of money, but that's not what success is all about.

"I think the answer comes down to character, which is certainly something you take

*Thomas A. Saunders III, class of
'58, went from VMI to Wall Street,
by way of the Darden School of
Business at the University of
Virginia, and now heads his own
investment firm with offices on
Madison Avenue, overlooking
Central Park.*

❖

"I think the answer comes down to character, which is certainly something you take away from VMI. The question you have to ask is: 'how do you conduct your business . . . your life?' In my business, you are only as good as your word. If you are on the telephone, doing a transaction that is worth millions of dollars, and you say you are going to do something, then you have to be good for it. I never had to be told that. I already knew it. Everyone who goes to VMI knows it.

"I was speaking at VMI on ethics not long ago, and I asked this question of the Corps, 'If someone has lied to you, have you ever forgotten it?' The point I was making is—when the dust settles, all you really have is your reputation."

Saunders has become a vastly successful New York financier, but he has not forgotten the institutions that enabled him to take advantage of his opportunities. "I believe if you are fortunate enough to be standing at the right stop when the right bus comes along—then you have a strong obligation to give something back." In that spirit, he has given generously to VMI—more than ten million dollars to promote merit-based scholarship which he believes will enable the Institute to attract and keep the kind of outstanding cadets it needs. Saunders has also given about fifteen million dollars to the Darden School at the University of Virginia for the establishment of the Saunders Center for Executive Education, and where the focal point of the new Darden Grounds is Saunders Hall.

Saunders gives of his time as well as his money. He has served on the VMI Foundation board and is currently a member of the Board of Visitors. While serving in this latter capacity, Saunders was deeply involved in the difficult days following the Supreme Court decision when the Board considered whether to comply with the decision and admit women, or to go private in an effort to keep things as they had always been.

"The Board's decision," says Saunders, "was tougher than any deal I have ever done. Deals are not emotional events. Everyone involved with VMI's decision felt very deeply about this special place and they presented their views with great conviction. I urged that we take a realistic view of the future and seize the high moral ground. Our obligation—painful as it was—was to take VMI into the twenty-first century and make it a truly unique place where a few young men and women can come for an educational and life experience that they cannot get anywhere else. If we accomplish this, VMI will continue to make an extraordinary contribution to the nation and remain the special place it has always been."

So, in the end, Saunders voted with the (bare) majority in favor of admitting women.

"We live in a world of remarkable and often unnerving change," says Saunders, who led the $150 billion AT&T divestiture after another famous court ruling, and perhaps knows a little something about how to cope with sudden, dramatic change. "One lesson I learned on Wall Street that has stood me in good stead throughout VMI's ordeal is to look at facts unemotionally, to measure risk and reward, and then make a decision.

"What we need to do now is close ranks, put our anguish behind us, keep VMI traditions and history in proper perspective, and look to the future as one of great opportunity."

Clark King

C lark King may be remembered with more affection by more cadets than anyone who has ever been associated with VMI. There are certainly thousands of men who remember—as vividly as they remember anything—Coach King's boxing course and what you had to do to earn an A.

"He'd tell you," says a man who took the famous course, "'if you want an A, I have got to see the blood.'"

King, retired since 1991, nods and smiles. He likes that story, too. "You'd see these kids come in here, and they didn't have any confidence. They had never been hurt and they had certainly never hurt anybody. So we worked on technique. Your stance, your guard, jabs and combinations, and so forth. It was like any other physical education class; it was for conditioning. Then, the last three weeks of the course, we boxed for a grade. The first week, they'd be so scared they wouldn't remember anything, they'd just go out there and flail around or cover up. They got better the second week. By the third week, the fear was all gone . . . you'd see such a tremendous change. I'd ask them if it hurt as much as they thought it would and most of them . . . they just laughed."

Everyone at VMI knew Coach King cared about the cadets—and the individual cadet—profoundly. They also knew that he understood something about handling life's challenges. King had been wounded (in the head) on Iwo Jima as a young Marine platoon leader a few days after taking over "a unit of twenty men that had started out as thirty-nine and by the time it was over, was down to seven or eight."

King was evacuated to a hospital ship. "We waited until it filled up—which didn't take long—then we went to Guam and back to the States." He was awarded a Silver Star.

After the war King, who had earned a degree from Gustavus Adolphus College in Minnesota, studied for a masters at the University of Wyoming. (He added an Ed.D. degree from the University of Virginia to his resume while he was at VMI.) King was coaching at a high school in his native state of Nebraska in 1950 when he was called back for Korea. In the end he never left Lejeune, but because he was on the east coast, he interviewed for a job at VMI as assistant football coach. He stayed at VMI for the next thirty-eight years as coach, teacher, inspiration, mentor, and father figure to class after class of cadets.

Those cadets remember Coach King for more than the legendary boxing course with its unique grading system. King introduced what has become the Rat Challenge program— the confidence course that blends Outward Bound training with Marine Corps obstacle course techniques. It has become a fixture at VMI, and the way it's run reflects King's belief in the young men he worked with. "I had a colonel from West Point come down and observe our program and he said, 'This is great but I'd have to put a Captain in charge. You've got cadets running it.' I told him that was the point."

On the trophy wall of King's home is a letter from one of the cadets who ran the Rat Challenge program. It reads: "I suppose all things have to come to an end . . . I'm happy in one way that it's over, but sad in another way. Running up that mountain twice a week can get rough, but I have to admit that I've enjoyed it, and that it's been the most rewarding experience of my life. It's a great feeling to know that you have enough confidence in my character and ability to put me in charge . . . For you, Dr. King, I will

Clark King came to VMI after service in the Marines, on Iwo Jima. He was coach, mentor, advisor, role model, and father figure to countless cadets in his thirty-eight years of service to the Institute.

❖

do anything within my power. So, to you, I give my sincere thanks. Call on me, *anytime.*"

Asked if any of the cadets he coached and influenced so deeply stay in touch, King says, simply, "All the time. I've got a couple of extra bedrooms downstairs for when they come by with their families. They were very, very good to me. I never had a day when I didn't want to go to work. It was tough to leave."

Asked what he misses the most, he shakes his head. "I don't know . . . a copier and a secretary."

And, while King has retired, he hasn't really left. He is back for the parades and for all the occasions when men return to VMI to be among their BRs. Though he never was a cadet at VMI, Coach King was made an honorary alumnus in a ceremony at Moody Hall in April of 1997. These days, when you see him on the parade ground, King is inevitably surrounded by men who want him to meet their wives and children, and who always introduce him in the same respectful tone. "This man," you'll hear them say, "had more influence on me than any man, except my father, in my whole life."

Heriot (Rhett) Clarkson

No man who goes through VMI finds it "easy," though it is less difficult for some, and almost impossibly difficult for others. Some of the men who have the toughest time getting through leave with the strongest sense of loyalty to the Institute. Rhett Clarkson is quick to characterize himself as one of those.

"It was nip and tuck all the way," he says. "Right up until the end, I didn't think I would ever make it. But VMI has a tremendous support system that works best for people like me and if there was any way they could make it happen, they were going to assist me in graduating."

He was, in a way, the ultimate first class private; one of those men who hold no rank but who are, in a real sense, the backbone of the Corps. In Clarkson's case, he was such a good first class private that he did it twice. "I struggled academically, the whole way. All my Brother Rats were class of '61 but I was a Bull Rat, back the next year, taking the courses I needed to graduate. I had to go through a little extra harassment for that, and it was a little lonely since you are so strong with your class at VMI. But, then, I got invited to a reunion by the class of '62 and considered it a very high honor."

He majored in civil engineering and became one of General James Morgan's "projects." "He took as much interest in me as he did in his best students. Maybe more." Clarkson was in despair of ever finishing the required courses and had almost given up when Morgan encouraged him to enroll in one last summer school course, at North Carolina State.

"I was all set to enlist in the army when General Morgan told me about that one course I needed for graduation. I think he was even happier than I was when I got a 'B.' I'll never forget the way he and other faculty members at VMI stood by me. I'd have never made it otherwise."

He could have taken a regular commission in the army but after agonizing over the decision, he turned it down. "My father was an Episcopal chaplain in the army and I knew military life. I had considered West Point and turned it down to go to VMI even though I'd never seen VMI before I went there. I liked the military but was not sure I wanted to stay in for a career."

Still, he served as a reserve officer. "I went to Korea. I was stationed there when JFK was shot."

After he left the army, the hard work it had taken to get through VMI began to pay off in the form of "the VMI alumni network." Clarkson went to work for a company in Verona, Virginia, surveying bridges. "The company was owned by a VMI graduate. I got the job as a result of VMI contacts. Coincidentally, I lived in New Market when I was working in that position."

He moved to another job with a firm in Richmond, also owned by a VMI graduate. "I learned about manufacturing concrete products there," he says. "And one night, I was playing cards with another VMI graduate and I said, 'We ought to go into the manhole business.'"

The other VMI graduate went on to graduate school but Clarkson found another partner and formed his new business. He had found his calling—entrepreneur and salesman—and if he'd had to struggle while at VMI, he was adroit at business.

"Some of it was luck—I caught the northern Virginia building boom at exactly the right time—and some of it was hard work. And . . . some of it was things that I had learned at VMI. Perseverance, mainly."

The company that had started out as an idea thrown out over cards was doing sixteen million in business by 1989. Clarkson sold the company in August, 1989 to an international conglomerate and remains an active consultant.

"I give all the credit to the people who believed in me and stood by me. And I try to give something back. I've raised money for VMI athletics and for other needs. I've given an athletic scholarship to the school in memory of my father. I served as President of the Keydet Club in the late '70s, served on the Board of Governors of the VMI Foundation and, of course, I'm now serving on the Board of Visitors. Lately, that has been challenging due to the recent court case and the preparation for the assimilation of women into VMI. I believe we fought the good fight and we have to go on. Maybe we'll make it the best coed school in the country.

"But I still believe the courts missed something very important about VMI. It is a successful school and its best work is with students like me in an all male environment. Students who might have slipped through the cracks some other place get the attention and the support . . . the caring at VMI that they need and that turns them into productive, responsible men and citizens."

Mrs. Wiley Wheat

The VMI family extends far across both country and generations, and includes not just the brotherhood of current and former cadets, but the people who are their families as well. Mrs. Wiley Wheat is as much a part of the VMI family as any man who ever walked the Ratline. In 1948 she married James C. Wheat '41, one of VMI's most remarkable graduates. "Many of Jim's classmates served in the war . . . and a number of them were lost. Three of Jim's closest friends were killed."

Rhett Clarkson, class of '61, was a first class private who became a member of the Board of Visitors and a successful businessman. He lives in Richmond.

❖

Mrs. Wiley Wheat is a loyal and longtime friend of the Institute. Her husband, James Wheat, was a distinguished graduate.

❖

James Wheat, however, was not eligible for war service. Though he had made it through VMI, he had in fact been going blind for a good part of his stay there: "He was always getting demerits for things that were the result of his bad sight. When they were in ranks, he could barely see the man in front of him. He had to memorize where things were and then he could remember how many steps he needed to take and so forth."

It was still very difficult. But Wheat persevered and made it through. He taught at the Institute during the war and then left in 1946 to start Wheat Securities, a brokerage that would soon become one of the largest in the South. "His first partner was a VMI man," Mrs. Wheat remembers. "He always liked hiring boys from VMI."

James Wheat enjoyed his success and lived to the full, in spite of losing his sight. "Oh, he never quit doing the things he loved to do. He hunted ducks and rode horses using other people for his eyes. They told him where to shoot and what to look out for. When he had to quit shooting ducks, he became a wonderful caller. He never felt sorry for himself. Never used a cane or a dog. He said learning how to use Braille was the hardest thing he ever did."

The Wheats were frequent visitors to VMI. James Wheat endowed a chair in economics, established a scholarship in memory of his father for cadets who wanted to go on to business school, and spoke at commencement on his fiftieth reunion. He was visiting VMI the night before he died, in 1992. "We knew Si Bunting back when he was still a cadet. He played the piano beautifully. And I remember that when he graduated, my son caught Si's shako."

Mrs. Wheat lives in a stately, two-hundred-year-old plantation on the Rappahannock River, but still travels back to Lexington: "I was there for Jim's fifty-fifth reunion," she says. "I saw Jim's Brother Rats and there are always so many good memories. It has meant so much to all of us, all these years."

Afterword

❖

On April 26, 1997, I reviewed the Alumni parade by the VMI Corps of Cadets. I have reviewed—and marched in—many parades at VMI and the ritual is always, more or less, the same. But on this day, the Corps, on its own, did something different. In a symbolic gesture, to honor the traditions of VMI and to acknowledge the challenges to come, the first class officers stuck their sabers into the ground, placed their shakos on top, and read the following proclamation. It seems a fitting valedictory to both this book and to an era:

General Bunting, distinguished alumni, ladies and gentlemen:

The officers of the Corps this year would like to commemorate the passing into history of VMI's all male cadet Corps. We recognize that VMI is about to undertake a brave new mission with the assimilation of women beginning with the '97–'98 academic year. In facing this opportunity, we believe that VMI will succeed in that mission and will show the country just what the VMI community is capable of.

The officers, in speaking for the Corps at large, would also like to commemorate the 157 years of VMI as an all-male military college. These 157 years will always be in the Institute's history and it is only right that we, as cadets and future alumni, recognize this fact and show pride in it. We wish to commemorate and pay tribute to VMI's history as an all-male military college and especially to the alumni who came before us, who have supported VMI wholeheartedly during the last few years. The days of struggle are over . . . VMI will be the most successful military college to assimilate women into its corps of cadets!

Gentlemen, we salute you and the Institute which you all represent. We do the following to recognize the bright future ahead of VMI and at the same time, to recognize and to remember . . . the last all male military college in the United States, our beloved Institute.

Thank you and Rah Virginia Mil!

Josiah Bunting III
May 15, 1997

VMI: A History

1836: Virginia legislature votes to organize a military school at Lexington Arsenal.

1837: Claudius Crozet appointed president of first Board of Visitors. Serves until 1845.

1839: Institute opens November 11, with twenty-eight cadets enrolled and Francis Henney Smith as principal professor.

1841: Francis Smith named first Superintendent. Faculty expanded to three.

1842: First cadets graduate and form Alumni Association.

1846: Twenty-six VMI graduates see military service during Mexican War.

1851: Thomas Jonathan Jackson joins faculty of VMI as professor of natural and experimental philosophy — physics — and artillery tactics. For his eccentricities, he is called by his students "Tom Fool Jackson." Later, the world will know him as "Stonewall Jackson."

1851: Construction completed on original barracks.

1859: Cadets ordered to provide security at execution of John Brown.

1861: As Civil War breaks out, the Corps is ordered to Richmond. Cadets serve as drill instructors and train some 15,000 men.

1863: On the eve of Chancellorsville, the battle that would be considered his greatest triumph, Jackson remarks, referring to the number of men in his command who are products of VMI: "The Institute will be heard from today." He is wounded in the battle, dies several days later, and is buried in Lexington.

1864: The Corps is called to serve as a reserve by General John Breckinridge, who faces a strong Union effort in the Valley. In the Battle of New Market, the Corps fills a gap in the Confederate lines and captures a Union field piece at a cost of ten dead and forty-seven wounded. A month later, a Union army retaliates by shelling and burning VMI.

1865: VMI reopens in makeshift quarters.

1865: Reconstruction completed on barracks, mess hall, and other buildings. VMI alumni purchase shoulder arms for Corps as U.S. Congress and President Grant look the other way.

1889: Major General Francis Smith, builder and rebuilder of VMI, retires after fifty years.

1890: Brigadier General Scott Shipp (he had added another "p" to his name since leading the Cadets at New Market) becomes second Superintendent.

1906: Sir Moses Ezekiel's statue honoring the New Market cadets —*Virginia Mourning Her Dead*—is dedicated on the grounds of VMI.

1915: Jackson Memorial Hall erected with federal funds provided by U.S. Congress in restitution for Civil War damages.

1918: Over eighty-five percent of VMI alumni between the ages of seventeen and forty serve in the armed forces during World War I. Fifty-seven are killed in action. One-hundred-thirty-eight are wounded. A total of 127 combat decorations are awarded to VMI men.

1919: Army ROTC formally established at VMI; one hundred horses arrive for mounted drill.

1921: Samuel W. Washington, Jr. becomes the first Rhodes Scholar from VMI.

1926: Ring Figure ceremony inaugurated.

1929: Major General John Archer Lejeune becomes fifth Superintendent.

1936: Major General Charles Evans Kilbourne, class of 1894, becomes sixth Superintendent. *Brother Rat* opens on Broadway.

1939: VMI celebrates its centennial with the dedication of Preston Library.

1941: More than four thousand VMI men serve in the armed forces during World War II, including fifty general officers, among them General of the Army George C. Marshall, Army Chief of Staff.

1949: New Barracks opens.

1950: More than two thousand VMI alumni serve in the armed forces during the Korean War. Twenty-six are killed in action.

1953: Secretary of State George C. Marshall (1901) awarded Nobel Peace Prize.

1962: A VMI graduate is one of the first U.S. soldiers killed in Vietnam. By the end of the war, forty-two other VMI men will be KIA.

1967: New Market Battlefield Park, a state park owned and administered by VMI, is open to the public.

1989: Major General John Williams Knapp becomes twelfth Superintendent.

1991: Two VMI men are killed in action during Operation Desert Storm.

1995: Educator, novelist and Rhodes scholar Josiah Bunting (1963) named thirteenth Superintendent.

1996: United States Supreme Court rules that VMI must admit qualified women applicants.

Above:

Medals won by Lewis "Chesty" Puller— including five Navy Crosses and one Distinguished Service Cross. Puller attended VMI for one year before becoming the most decorated U.S. Marine in history. From the VMI Museum.

Glossary

BDUs (Battle Dress Uniform): Camouflage fatigues worn for forced marches and other military functions.

bone: To report a cadet for an infraction of the rules. Get your name on the bone sheet often enough and you will find yourself walking PTs.

BRC: Breakfast Roll Call. The first formation of the day.

break starch: To step into a fresh, stiff pair of white ducks.

Breakout: The last step for fourth classmen, the one that breaks the chains of the Ratline.

BRF: A pejorative used to describe a cadet who takes advantage of—or ignores the needs of—his Brother Rats.

Brother Rat: The men with whom you matriculated. Also, a form of address usually in anticipation of some loan or favor, i.e.: "Brother Rat, can you spare me ten?"

BRs: Short for "Brother Rats."

Bull Rat: A fifth year man.

The Bullet: The Rat Bible. The text. Rats will know the information in its pages…or pay.

cadre: The cadets responsible for teaching the Rats their right from their left and other fundamentals of life at VMI. Cadet officers and non-coms chosen for their military qualities.

CQ: Call to Quarters. All cadets must be in barracks.

CCQ: Closed Call to Quarters. In barracks and in your room.

coatee: Dress gray coat with brass buttons. Worn for ceremonial occasions.

Commandant (Commandant of Cadets): Administration officer responsible for cadet discipline and barracks life and routine.

the Corps: The cadets of VMI, as a unit.

CP: Command Post

CQRB: Call to Quarters with Release in Barracks. In barracks, with some activity permitted outside your room.

crossed dykes: Crossed white belts worn with coatee, especially for parades.

Dark Ages, the: After Christmas and before Breakout. The time of short days and long nights. Most depressing time of year.

DRC: Dinner Roll Call. Mid-day formation, after which the Corps marches to the mess hall for lunch.

drum out: The dismissal of a cadet found guilty of an honor code violation. Named for the long roll of drums which precedes the announcement.

Dyke (person): First classman designated as a Rat's mentor. Also applied within the relationship to the Rat himself.

dyke (clothing and verb): Uniform, or to put on one. As in, "class dyke," "gym dyke," "dyke out," etc.

EC: (The Executive Committee): Subcommittee of General Committee which deals with serious cases of discipline and conduct in Barracks.

EMT: Emergency medical technician.

flamers: Those cadets who seem to take delight in the suffering of Rats. The hard cases. To "flame" is to yell at a Rat or to "light him up."

GC: (The General Committee): Group responsible for standards and appearance of Corps. Headed by president of first class. Includes all class officers and president of the OGA. RDC, EC, and OGA are subcommittees of the GC.

gim: The sick list. A cadet who is routinely excused from duty for medical reasons is said to be "riding the gim."

hay: What passes, at VMI, for a bed.

JM Hall: Jackson Memorial Hall. The chapel and site of important assemblies.

Minks: Students of neighboring Washington and Lee University.

OD: Officer of the Day. The cadet in charge of the guard team. Only cadet required to bone anyone caught violating rules. Hence, his habit of jangling keys to warn of his approach.

OGA (Officers of the Guard Association): Comprised of all first class privates, this group is responsible for morale in barracks and reports to the first class president.

Old Corps: Those cadets who are not Rats. Upper classmen. Also, those VMI men who are no longer cadets but can still remember what it was like when they were.

on the bricks: The pavement in front of Old Barracks. The old bricks are still there, covered by asphalt, but can still be seen outside of Washington Arch, on the east face of Old Barracks.

penalty tour (PT): A one hour march, on the bricks, which serves as punishment for an excess demerit.

permit worms: Cadets, especially Rats, whose involvement in extra-curricular activities excuses them from the rigorous, military side of barracks life.

Pervert corner, Gold Coast, Ghetto: Sections of the Old Barracks so designated because of cadet activities and behavior in the past.

pugil stick: Imitation rifle, padded at both ends, used for bayonet practice. Good for working off the tensions of barracks life.

rack: Synonym for "hay." Technically, the cot upon which the mattress (the "hay") rests.

Rat: The lowest form of life and so on and so forth.

Rat Bible: **The Bullet.** The book which contains the rules, regulations, and essential knowledge for all Rats.

Rat Daddies: Upper classmen who take pity on helpless Rats and protect them, when possible, from the "flamers."

Rat Mass: The collectivity of Rats. They do not yet have the unity to be called a class, and won't, until Breakout when they become, officially, the newest class at VMI.

Ratline: Technically, the imaginary line in barracks from which Rats must not deviate as they move about. In actual use—the entire scope of Rat discipline.

RDC (Rat Disciplinary Committee): First classmen dedicated to enforcing discipline and standards among the Rats. Inquisitors who meet in dark, subterranean rooms.

Resurrection: The period just prior to Breakout.

Ring Figure: The most important social weekend of the VMI year, when second classmen get their rings and, as part of the ceremony, spell out their class number, in formation, on the dance floor.

rolled, to be: To be drummed out, expelled from VMI. Comes from the sound of the drum roll that precedes the announcement of the president of the Honor Court.

Sally port: The passageway that connects Old and New Barracks.

shakos: Dress headgear.

the sinks: Technically, the bathrooms. In use, the area below the first stoop which includes rooms where first classmen and fifth year men live. So called because this was where all the bathrooms were in the old days. Incidentally, this expression dates back to the days of the arsenal, making it one of oldest slang terms still in use at VMI.

smack Rats: Rats who are insufficiently serious.

SRC: Supper Roll Call. Last formation of the day.

stoop: Floor of the barracks, i.e., first stoop, second stoop, etc. Also the balcony area on each floor.

Supe (Superintendent): The man. The General. The head of the school.

TAC: Tactical Officer. A member of the administration, assigned to Barracks, known for making rounds and performing bed checks after hours when some cadets may be running the block. Arm of the Commandant.

Tech: Virginia Technical Institute, a nearby school for engineering.

W&L: Washington & Lee. Liberal arts university on the other side of Limits Gate.

woollies: Gray wool pants worn by cadets for four years, then burned by first classmen in a rite of spring.

Acknowledgments

This book began, seven years ago, in a conversation between Anthony Edgeworth and Colonel John Ripley, U.S.M.C., who was then in command of the NROTC unit at VMI. Edgeworth had published books on the Marines and the British Guards Regiments, so VMI seemed like a natural subject. The aim would be to capture the essence of the Institute in photographs taken over the course of a single year.

What separates VMI—what makes it unique—is, of course, its austerity and rigor. The institute offers what students can get at many schools—a quality education and a strong athletic program, but at those other schools, there is no reveille and students do not march to meals. There is, of course, no Ratline. VMI students choose the harder, Spartan path (and pay for the privilege, unlike those who attend the service academies) and this seems the soul of VMI and what Edgeworth wanted to capture in photographs.

A sense of tradition is, of course, one of VMI's strengths. It has not, in its long history, been subject to change. One year is much like the next. After languishing for some time, the project was revived with the enthusiastic support, blessing, and encouragement of Superintendent Josiah Bunting. To say that this book would not have been possible except for his efforts would be to vastly understate the case. So the project was launched, formally, on New Market Day, May 15, 1996, with Bunting as walking point. Edgeworth (and writer Geoffrey Norman) would follow life at VMI from then, into the summer, when the cadets were on ROTC summer duty, and through the following year, concluding on New Market day 1997.

By sheer coincidence, it was to be a year unlike any other in the Institute's history: the year of the Supreme Court decision, the last year when VMI would be an all-male school.

Still, the objective of this book was always to capture the essential, unchanging soul of VMI; the routines and rituals of life in the barracks and on the Post. The aim was to record, as vividly and faithfully as possible, a way of life that seems quaint, at best, to outsiders, and is cherished by those who have experienced it. This book was meant to be a record—and a celebration— of the life and the history of this unique institution.

In a year when those with an interest in VMI had many other things on their minds, we were treated by everyone connected to the Institute with unfailing courtesy and generosity. Many people have gone out of their way to help us during the making of this book, and we would like to thank them all.

Special mention should be made of some. Superintendent Bunting, who made all things possible, and his wife Diana. Samuel B. Witt III. Colonel Ed Dooley. Colonel Roy Hammond. Colonel Keith Gibson, Colonel Al Farrell, Colonel Mike Stickler. Colonel Keith Dickson, Sergeant-Major Al Hockaday U.S.M.C. (Ret). Cadets Brian Bagwan, Addison Hagan, and Jeffrey Staub. Cadet Taylor Edwards who was both guide and literary advisor, as well as his BRs down in the sinks. Patsy Smith and Lori Parrent in the Superintendent's office, who must have wondered, from time to time, when they had adopted us. Magaret Jones at Moody Hall. Richard L. Sutton, friend and legal sage. John and Molin Ripley, who supplied hospitality in Lexington.

During our year at VMI, our access was unlimited; our questions answered with frankness and candor; our requests—no matter how unusual or unorthodox—invariably and promptly granted. We were made to feel, in short, a part of the VMI family. What began as a professional undertaking became, very quickly, a labor of love. It is impossible to be at VMI very long— among the cadets, administrators, and alumni—without sharing some of the pride and loyalty that has sustained the Institute so well. We hope that some measure of that feeling is conveyed in the pages of this book.

Anthony Edgeworth
Geoffrey Norman
May, 1997